A BALANCED MATHEMATICS PROGRAM INTEGRATING SCIENCE AND LANGUAGE ARTS

Unit Resource Guide
Unit 7
Decimals and Probability

THIRD EDITION

KENDALL/HUNT PUBLISHING COMPANY
4050 Westmark Drive   Dubuque, Iowa 52002

A TIMS® Curriculum
University of Illinois at Chicago

Carta al hogar

Decimales y probabilidad

Fecha: _____

Estimado miembro de familia:

En esta unidad, su hijo/a aprenderá que las fracciones, los decimales y los porcentajes pueden describir la misma cantidad (por ejemplo, $\frac{1}{4} = 0.25 = 25\%$). Los estudiantes también trabajarán con el valor posicional de decimales y harán cálculos con decimales.

Leer etiquetas ayuda a los estudiantes a aprender acerca de decimales y porcentajes

A medida que exploremos los decimales y las fracciones, estudiaremos las probabilidades relacionadas con echar una moneda al aire. La probabilidad se usa a menudo en la vida cotidiana, en todos los ámbitos, desde el pronóstico del tiempo hasta los deportes; pero no siempre se entiende correctamente. Nuestras investigaciones ayudarán a los estudiantes a entender este tema.

Puede ayudar a su hijo/a en casa haciendo lo siguiente:

• Señalando decimales y porcentajes en la vida cotidiana. Los encontrará en etiquetas de comida, productos de limpieza, anuncios, páginas deportivas, calculadoras, odómetros de automóviles, y muchos otros lugares.

• Ayudando a su hijo a repasar las tablas de multiplicación y división. Puede usar las *tarjetas triangulares* para repasar las tablas.

Por favor, comuníquese conmigo si tiene alguna pregunta, inquietud o comentario sobre esta unidad.

Atentamente,

_____

Table of Contents

Unit 7
Decimals and Probability

Unit 7

Outline
Decimals and Probability

Unit Summary

Estimated Class Sessions
13-18

A major goal of this unit is to help students understand that often they can express a quantity as a fraction, decimal, and a percent. Students use two models to help them make connections between fractions and decimal symbols: centiwheels (circles divided into hundredths) and squares divided into tenths, hundredths, and thousandths.

Students work with these grids to reinforce place value concepts, compare decimals, round decimals, and model addition and subtraction of decimals. They use an area model to learn to place decimals in products of decimal multiplication problems. Students use their knowledge of decimals to explore probabilities.

They complete a lab, *Flipping Two Coins,* in which they explore the results of coin flipping experiments. The lab is related to a real-life story in the Adventure Book *Unlikely Heroes.* The DPP for this unit reviews all the multiplication and division facts.

Major Concept Focus

- reading and writing decimals
- multiplication and division facts
- decimal place value
- rounding decimals
- adding decimals
- comparing decimals
- multiplying decimals
- subtracting decimals
- using fractions to write probabilities
- estimating with decimals
- using decimals to write probabilities
- probabilities of flipping coins
- *Adventure Book:* probability
- law of large numbers
- bar graphs
- TIMS Laboratory Method
- relationships between fractions, decimals, and percents
- predictions from graphs

Pacing Suggestions

This unit extends the study of fractions to decimals and probability. If students had experiences with decimals and probability in earlier grades, use the smaller of the recommended number of sessions to guide your planning. If students have not previously worked with decimals, they will move more slowly through the lessons. However, it is not necessary to wait until all students have mastered all the skills, as they will use them in later units in new contexts and continue to practice them in the Daily Practice and Problems and Home Practice. In particular, Unit 8 *Applications: An Assessment Unit* reviews fractions, decimals, and percents.

- Omit Part 1 of Lesson 1 if your students have studied decimals before. This optional part of the lesson, *A Review: Tenths and Hundredths,* introduces decimals using base-ten pieces. The material is from third and fourth grades.
- Lesson 9 *Families with Two Children* is an optional lesson that can serve as an extension. The activity is a real-world application of probability.

Assessment Indicators

Use the following Assessment Indicators and the *Observational Assessment Record* that follows the Background section in this unit to assess students on key ideas.

A1. Can students represent decimals using centi-wheels and decimal grids?

A2. Can students use fractions, decimals, and percents to represent the same quantity?

A3. Can students read and write decimals to thousandths?

A4. Can students compare and order decimals?

A5. Can students add and subtract decimals?

A6. Can students multiply decimals?

A7. Can students collect, organize, graph, and analyze data?

A8. Can students make and interpret bar graphs?

A9. Can students use fractions and percents to give the probability of an event?

Unit Planner

KEY: SG = Student Guide, DAB = Discovery Assignment Book, AB = Adventure Book, URG = Unit Resource Guide, DPP = Daily Practice and Problems, HP = Home Practice (found in Discovery Assignment Book), and TIG = Teacher Implementation Guide.

	Lesson Information	Supplies	Copies/Transparencies
Lesson 1 **Fractions, Decimals, and Percents** URG Pages 29–58 SG Pages 222–229 DAB Page 101 DPP A–D HP Parts 1–3 *Estimated Class Sessions* **2-3**	**Activity** Students explore the relationship between fractions, decimals, and percents. An optional part of the activity from Grades 3 and 4 is included for students with little experience with decimals. **Math Facts** DPP item C reviews math facts. **Homework** 1. Students complete homework *Questions 1–5* in the *Student Guide*. 2. Students complete the *Designing Quilts* Homework Page in the *Discovery Assignment Book*. They will use their quilt designs in Lesson 2. 3. Assign Parts 1 and 2 of the Home Practice in the *Discovery Assignment Book*. **Assessment** Use Part 3 of the Home Practice as a quiz.	• 1 pair of scissors per student • 1 hole punch per student, optional • 1 set of base-ten pieces (2 flats, 20 skinnies, 15 bits) per student pair, optional	• 1 copy of *Tenths and Hundredths* URG Pages 42–47 per student, optional • 1 copy of *Centiwheel Disks* URG Page 48 per student, 1 disk on colored paper and 1 disk on white paper • 1 small disk from *Small Centiwheels* URG Page 49 per student • 2 copies of *Three-trial Data Table* URG Page 50 per student • 1 copy of *Centiwheel Disks* URG Page 48, 1 enlarged disk on white paper and 1 enlarged disk on colored paper for demonstration, optional
Lesson 2 **Decimal Models** URG Pages 59–77 SG Pages 230–237 DAB Page 103 DPP E–F HP Part 4 *Estimated Class Sessions* **1-2**	**Activity** Students use an area model to review tenths, hundredths, and thousandths. They use a place value chart to help them read and write decimals. **Homework** 1. Assign the questions in the Homework section in the *Student Guide*. Students will need a *Decimal Grids* Activity Page to complete the homework. 2. Assign the game *Score One*. 3. Assign Part 4 of the Home Practice. **Assessment** Use some of the homework questions as an assessment.	• 1 pair of scissors per student, optional • 1 toothpick per student, optional	• 2 copies of *Decimal Grids* URG Page 70 per student • 1 transparency of *Decimal Place Value Chart* URG Page 69, optional • 1 transparency of *Decimal Grids* URG Page 70, optional
Lesson 3 **Comparing and Rounding Decimals** URG Pages 78–93 SG Pages 238–242 DAB Pages 105–111 DPP G–J HP Part 5 *Estimated Class Sessions* **2**	**Activity** Students compare and order decimals using an area model and benchmark numbers of 0, 0.1, 0.5, and 1. They also use the area model to round decimals to the nearest whole number, tenth, and hundredth. **Math Facts** DPP item G reviews the multiplication and division facts. **Homework** 1. Assign the Homework section in the *Student Guide*. Students will need a copy of the *Decimal Grids* Activity Page from the *Unit Resource Guide* to complete the assignment. 2. Assign the *Connect the Dots* Activity Page in the *Discovery Assignment Book* for homework. (optional) **Assessment** Use Part 5 of the Home Practice as a quiz.		• 1–3 copies of *Decimal Grids* URG Page 70 per student • 1 transparency of *Decimals: A Closer Look* DAB Pages 105–109, optional • 1 transparency of *Decimal Place Value Chart* URG Page 69 • 1 transparency of *Decimal Grids* URG Page 70

	Lesson Information	Supplies	Copies/ Transparencies
Lesson 4 **Adding and Subtracting Decimals** URG Pages 94–106 SG Pages 243–246 DAB Pages 113–118 DPP K–L *Estimated Class Sessions* **1-2**	**Activity** Students use their knowledge of place value to align numbers correctly and then solve addition and subtraction problems with decimals. **Math Facts** DPP item K reviews math facts. **Homework** Assign *Questions 1–10* in the Homework section on the *Adding and Subtracting Decimals* Activity Pages in the *Student Guide* for homework. **Assessment** 1. Use *Questions 7–8* in the Homework section on the *Adding and Subtracting Decimals* Activity Pages in the *Student Guide* as an assessment. 2. Use DPP Task L as an assessment.		• 1 transparency of *Adding Decimals with Grids* DAB Page 113 • 1 transparency of *Subtracting Decimals with Grids* DAB Page 117 • 1 transparency of *Decimal Place Value Chart* URG Page 69
Lesson 5 **Multiplying Decimals with Area** URG Pages 107–116 SG Pages 247–251 DPP M–N HP Part 6 *Estimated Class Sessions* **1-2**	**Activity** Students investigate multiplying decimals. They develop a sense for the placement of a decimal in a product through estimation and the use of an area model. **Homework** 1. Assign the Homework section in the *Multiplying Decimals with Area* Activity Pages in the *Student Guide*. 2. Assign Part 6 of the Home Practice.	• 1 ruler per student	• 1–3 copies of *Centimeter Grid Paper* URG Page 113 per student • 1 transparency of *Centimeter Grid Paper* URG Page 113
Lesson 6 **Paper-and-Pencil Decimal Multiplication** URG Pages 117–125 SG Pages 252–254 DPP O–P *Estimated Class Sessions* **1**	**Activity** Students learn a procedure for placing decimals in products. **Math Facts** DPP Bit O reviews the multiplication and division facts. **Homework** Assign the Homework section in the *Student Guide*. **Assessment** Use the *Decimal Quiz* as an assessment of students' skills.		• 1 copy of *Decimal Quiz* URG Page 123 per student

(Continued)

	Lesson Information	**Supplies**	**Copies/ Transparencies**
Lesson 7 **Flipping One Coin** URG Pages 126–134 SG Pages 255–257 DPP Q–R HP Part 8 Estimated Class Sessions **1**	**Activity** Students flip a coin 40 times and count the number of times heads or tails show. The probability of flipping a head is discussed and compared to experimental results. **Homework** Assign Part 8 of the Home Practice in the *Discovery Assignment Book*.	• 1 penny per student group • 1 small paper cup per student group, optional • 1 small cloth for tossing coins to muffle the sound per student group, optional	• 1 copy of *Three-column Data Table* URG Page 132 per student, optional
Lesson 8 **Flipping Two Coins** URG Pages 135–153 SG Pages 258–264 DAB Pages 119–123 DPP S–X HP Part 7 Estimated Class Sessions **3**	**Lab** Students flip a penny and a nickel repeatedly and record the number of heads showing. Data is compared for 10, 100, and 1000 trials after pooling data with classmates. **Math Facts** DPP items S and W review the multiplication and division facts. **Homework** 1. *Questions 1–4* provide practice translating fractions, decimals, and percents. Assign these questions before students analyze their data. 2. Assign *Question 5* after students complete the lab. They play a game and use what they learned from the lab to decide if it is fair or unfair. 3. Assign Part 7 of the Home Practice. **Assessment** 1. Assign points to one or more sections of the lab and grade them as an assessment. 2. As students analyze their group data, record their abilities to make and interpret bar graphs on the *Observational Assessment Record*. 3. Transfer appropriate documentation to students' *Individual Assessment Record Sheets*	• 1 calculator per student group • 1 penny per student group • 1 nickel per student group • 1 small paper cup per student group, optional • 1 small cloth for tossing coins to muffle the sound per student group, optional	• 3 copies of *Centimeter Graph Paper* URG Page 147 per student • 1 transparency of *Coin Flipping Data Tables* DAB Page 121, optional • 1 copy of *Observational Assessment Record* URG Pages 13–14 to be used throughout this unit • 1 copy of *Individual Assessment Record Sheet* TIG Assessment section per student, previously copied for use throughout the year
Lesson 9 **Families with Two Children** URG Pages 154–158 SG Pages 265–267 Estimated Class Sessions **1**	OPTIONAL LESSON—EXTENSION **Optional Activity** Using ideas from the lab in Lesson 8, students investigate the probability that a family with two children will have 0, 1, or 2 boys. **Homework** Students collect data at home on two-children families.		

	Lesson Information	Supplies	Copies/ Transparencies
Lesson 10 **Unlikely Heroes** URG Pages 159–165 AB Pages 35–46 DPP Y–Z *Estimated Class Sessions* **1**	**Adventure Book** Students read a story about John Kerrich, an Englishman who was imprisoned in Denmark during World War II. Kerrich completed experiments involving probabilities of coin tosses while in prison.	• pennies, optional	

Preparing for Upcoming Lessons

Pennies will be needed for Lesson 7. Pennies and nickels will be needed for Lesson 8.

Save the interlocking centiwheels and the small centiwheels made in Lesson 1 for use in Units 8, 9, and 14.

Bubble solution and wands will be needed for Unit 8.

Connections

A current list of literature and software connections is available at *www.mathtrailblazers.com*. You can also find information or connections in the *Teacher Implementation Guide* Literature List and Software List sections.

Literature Connections
Suggested Titles
- Coffland, Jack & David. *Basketball Math.* Good Year Books, Tucson, AZ, 2002.
- Lowry, Lois. *Number the Stars.* Houghton Mifflin Co., Boston, MA, 1989. (Lesson 10)
- Smith, David J. *If the World Were a Village: A Book about the World's People.* Kids Can Press, Ltd., Tonawanda, NY, 2002.

Software Connections
- *Graph Master* allows students to collect data and create their own graphs.
- *Math Arena* is a collection of math activities that reinforces many math concepts.
- *Math Munchers Deluxe* provides practice in basic facts and finding equivalent fractions, decimals, percents, ratios, angles and identifying geometric shapes, factors, and multiples in an arcade-like game.
- *Mighty Math Calculating Crew* poses short answer questions about number operations, 3-dimensional shapes, and money skills.
- *Mighty Math Number Heroes* poses short answer questions about fractions, number operations, polygons, and probability.
- *National Library of Virtual Manipulatives* website (http://matti.usu.edu) allows students to work with manipulatives including geoboards, base-ten pieces, the abacus, and many others.
- *TinkerPlots* allows students to record, compare, and analyze data in tables and graphs.

Teaching All Math Trailblazers Students

Math Trailblazers® lessons are designed for students with a wide range of abilities. The lessons are flexible and do not require significant adaptation for diverse learning styles or academic levels. However, when needed, lessons can be tailored to allow students to engage their abilities to the greatest extent possible while building knowledge and skills.

To assist you in meeting the needs of all students in your classroom, this section contains information about some of the features in the curriculum that allow all students access to mathematics. For additional information, see the Teaching the *Math Trailblazers* Student: Meeting Individual Needs section in the *Teacher Implementation Guide.*

Differentiation Opportunities in this Unit

Games

Use games to promote or extend understanding of math concepts and to practice skills with children who need more practice.

- *Digits Game* from DPP Task F in Lesson 2 *Decimal Models*
- *Score One* from Lesson 2 *Decimal Models*
- *How Many Heads?* from Lesson 8 *Flipping Two Coins*
- *Matching 2 Pennies* from Lesson 8 *Flipping Two Coins*

Laboratory Experiments

Laboratory experiments enable students to solve problems using a variety of representations including pictures, tables, graphs, and symbols. Teachers can assign or adapt parts of the analysis according to the student's ability. The following lesson is a lab:

- Lesson 8 *Flipping Two Coins*

Journal Prompts

Journal prompts provide opportunities for students to explain and reflect on mathematical problems. They can help both students who need practice explaining their ideas and students who benefit from answering higher order questions. Students with various learning styles can express themselves using pictures, words, and sentences. Teachers can alter journal prompts to suit students' ability levels. The following lesson contains a journal prompt:

- Lesson 4 *Adding and Subtracting Decimals*

DPP Challenges

DPP Challenges are items from the Daily Practice and Problems that usually take more than fifteen minutes to complete. These problems are more thought-provoking and can be used to stretch students' problem-solving skills. The following lessons have a DPP Challenge in them:

- DPP Challenge N from Lesson 5 *Multiplying Decimals with Area*
- DPP Challenge X from Lesson 8 *Flipping Two Coins*

Background
Decimals and Probability

A major goal of this unit is to help students understand that the same quantity can often be expressed as a fraction, decimal, and percent. Most students do not recognize that decimals are often just a different way of writing fractions (Carpenter et al., 1981). To help students understand that decimals do not represent an entirely new quantitative system, they use fraction models to investigate those numbers easily represented by decimals.

Students will use two models to help them make connections between fractions and decimal symbols. They first use circles we call centiwheels. The centiwheel is divided into 100 equal segments around its outside edge. See Figure 1.

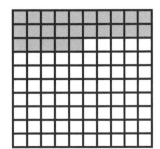

Figure 1: *Interlocking centiwheel disks model $\frac{1}{4}$, 0.25, and 25%.*

Students also use grids divided into tenths, hundredths, and thousandths. Figure 2 shows grids for hundredths and thousandths. These grids provide another means for making connections between fractions and decimals. Students also use the grids to compare decimals and to model addition and subtraction of decimals.

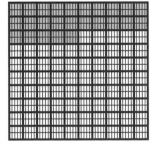

Figure 2: $\frac{25}{100} = 0.25$ and $\frac{250}{1000} = 0.250$

Both $\frac{25}{100}$ and 0.25 are fractions. Fractions like $\frac{25}{100}$ are called **common fractions** or just fractions. Fractions like 0.25 are called **decimal fractions** or just **decimals.** The context in which we use numbers often determines the most appropriate form to use. For instance, a story in the school newspaper about a recent basketball game may include information on the star player's shooting performance. If Shannon shot ten times and made four baskets, it is mathematically correct to report the fraction of successful shots with a common fraction, a decimal, or a percent as shown below.

- Using a common fraction: She made $\frac{4}{10}$ or $\frac{2}{5}$ of her shots.
- Using a decimal: She made 0.4 or 0.40 of her shots.
- Using a percent: She made 40% of her shots.

Each expression represents the same quantity. However, the way we use these numbers determines which representation we select. For example, decimals and percents are convenient to use when comparing two groups of different size. Suppose we want to compare the shooting performance for two different players: Shannon and Felicia. While Shannon made 4 out of 10 shots, Felicia made 3 out of 7. We can find a decimal (or decimal approximation) and then a percent for each common fraction. Since Shannon made $\frac{4}{10}$ of her shots, 0.40 or 40% of her shots were successful. Since Felicia made $\frac{3}{7}$ of her shots, about 0.43 or 43% of her shots were successful. Because we have essentially rewritten both of the common fractions with denominators of 100, comparisons are easier.

Using a decimal representation is often the most efficient way to find an answer when computation is needed to solve a problem. For example, efficient strategies for finding the area of a floor, which measures $8\frac{1}{2}$ ft by $7\frac{1}{2}$ ft include multiplying 8.5 by 7.5 using a calculator or a pencil-and-paper method.

Decimal Place Value and Computation

Another goal is to extend the understanding of the ten-to-one relationship of the base-ten place value system. In Unit 2 *Big Numbers,* students reviewed the concept that the value of each place in a whole number is ten times as great as the place to its right. This ten-to-one relationship extends to include numbers that are less than one. Places to the right of the decimal point have the same ten-to-one relationship: tenths, hundredths, thousandths, ten-thousandths, etc.

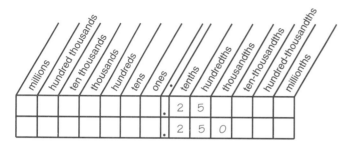

Figure 3: *Decimal place value chart*

One approach to addition and subtraction of decimals has its roots in understanding decimal place value. If children understand that they can do these operations correctly only when like places (columns) are aligned, the actual addition and subtraction will hold no mystery. "Developing procedures for the addition and subtraction of multidigit numbers, both whole numbers and decimal numbers, should involve the students' understanding of place value." (Hiebert and Carpenter, 1992) If students understand an addition or subtraction algorithm dependent on place value when working with whole numbers, then work with decimals should come easily. An area model is used to provide concrete experiences with decimal addition and subtraction.

Multiplication of decimals can be more complex than addition and subtraction. The traditional procedure for placing decimals in the product can have little meaning for children. In this unit, students learn to place the decimals in two ways: They combine an area model with a number sense perspective. Multiplying 8.5 by 7.5 is placed in the context of finding the area of a room. First students estimate that the area of an 8.5 ft by 7.5 ft room is between 56 sq ft and 72 sq ft. Then they find the area on grid paper as shown in Figure 4. With this background, children estimate the magnitude of the product of two decimals and use an algorithm of their choice to multiply. Then they use their estimation skills to place the decimal point correctly in the product. Through class discussion, students look for a pattern in the relationship between the number of decimal places in the factors and the number of decimal places in the product. Finally, they use the pattern to develop an efficient procedure for placing the decimal point in the product.

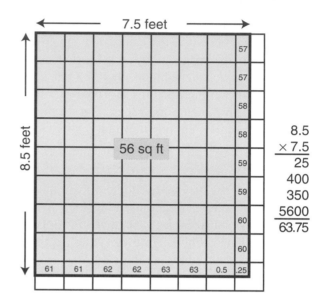

Estimate: 8.5 × 7.5 is between 56 and 72.

Figure 4: *Applying an area model and number sense to multiply decimals*

Probability

The activity, *Flipping One Coin,* and the lab, *Flipping Two Coins,* give students the opportunity to investigate the probabilities involved in coin flipping. Analyzing their data allows them to apply some of the skills they learned earlier in their study of decimals, fractions, and percents.

Students who used *Math Trailblazers* in earlier grades will have some background in probability. Many primary grade activities introduce students to sampling and random variation along with basic data collection and analysis. The first formal treatment of probability occurred in fourth grade, where students studied the probabilities involved in spinning spinners and rolling number cubes. However, students with little background in probability should still be able to do the activities in this unit.

Probability is a measure of how likely an event is to happen. A probability is a number from 0 to 1. Probabilities then can be expressed as fractions, decimals, and percents. Percents are more easily compared than fractions.

One of this unit's main ideas is that probabilities describe the behavior of systems *over the long run.* As the sample size grows, the behavior of the system more closely resembles that predicted by the underlying probabilities. This fact is sometimes called the Law of Large Numbers. For example, the probability that a head will come up when a coin is flipped is $\frac{1}{2}$. The Law of Large Numbers says that if we flip the coin many times, heads will come up about half the time. Although we do not discuss this law formally, students will observe its effects in the activity *Flipping One Coin.* The effects are also observed in the lab *Flipping Two Coins.* In this lab, students flip a nickel and a penny and count the number of times zero, one, and two heads show. There are four possible outcomes showing heads (H) and tails (T). These outcomes are HH, HT, TH, and TT, so the probabilities of getting zero heads (TT) and two heads (HH) are both $\frac{1}{4}$, while the probability of getting one head (HT or TH) is $\frac{2}{4}$ or $\frac{1}{2}$. Students will analyze their results after 10, 100, and 1000 two-coin flips. They will see that the percentages of 0, 1, and 2 head flips more closely resemble the probabilities after larger numbers of flips.

One of the most commonly held incorrect beliefs about probability relates to the Law of Large Numbers. Suppose a coin is being flipped repeatedly and has come up heads in all of the last several flips. Is the probability of a head on the next flip more than, less than, or equal to one half? The answer is that the probability is always equal to one half. Many people will say that since a coin is expected to come up heads about half the time in a large number of flips, it must be more likely to come up tails this next time because "we're due for a tail." But the coin has no memory. It doesn't know that it has just produced a long string of heads. With coin flipping, the Law of Large Numbers says that eventually the distribution will approach 50% heads and 50% tails (if the coin is fair). It does not say anything about any one flip.

There are other false notions about coin flipping that students will have an opportunity to correct. Some people believe heads will come up more often if the first toss shows a head. This is not true. Others believe that the surface the coin lands on or the person flipping affects whether heads or tails show. As long as the coin is flipped many times and is "fair" or balanced, the outcome depends on nothing but chance. Encourage students to investigate the validity of any of their own theories about coin flipping.

Resources

- Carpenter, Thomas P., et al. "Decimals: Results and Implications from National Assessment." *Arithmetic Teacher,* 28(8), pp. 34–37, National Council of Teachers of Mathematics, Reston, VA, 1981.

- Hiebert, J. "Research Report: Decimal Fractions." *Arithmetic Teacher,* 34(7), pp. 22–23, National Council of Teachers of Mathematics, Reston, VA, 1987.

- Hiebert, James, and Thomas P. Carpenter. "Learning and Teaching with Understanding." In *Handbook of Research on Mathematics Teaching and Learning,* ed. by D.A. Grouws, pp. 65–97. McMillan Publishing Company, New York, 1992.

- Van de Walle, John A. *Elementary and Middle School Mathematics: Teaching Developmentally.* Longman, White Plains, NY, 1998.

Observational Assessment Record

A1 Can students represent decimals using centiwheels and decimal grids?

A2 Can students use fractions, decimals, and percents to represent the same quantity?

A3 Can students read and write decimals to thousandths?

A4 Can students compare and order decimals?

A5 Can students add and subtract decimals?

A6 Can students multiply decimals?

A7 Can students collect, organize, graph, and analyze data?

A8 Can students make and interpret bar graphs?

A9 Can students use fractions and percents to give the probability of an event?

A10 _____

Name	A1	A2	A3	A4	A5	A6	A7	A8	A9	A10	Comments
1.											
2.											
3.											
4.											
5.											
6.											
7.											
8.											
9.											
10.											
11.											
12.											
13.											

Name	A1	A2	A3	A4	A5	A6	A7	A8	A9	A10	Comments
14.											
15.											
16.											
17.											
18.											
19.											
20.											
21.											
22.											
23.											
24.											
25.											
26.											
27.											
28.											
29.											
30.											
31.											
32.											

Unit 7

Daily Practice and Problems
Decimals and Probability

A DPP Menu for Unit 7

Two Daily Practice and Problems (DPP) items are included for each class session listed in the Unit Outline. A scope and sequence chart for the DPP is in the *Teacher Implementation Guide*.

Icons in the Teacher Notes column designate the subject matter of each DPP item. The first item in each class session is always a Bit and the second is either a Task or Challenge. Each item falls into one or more of the categories listed below. A menu of the DPP items for Unit 7 follows.

N Number Sense E, F, I, L–N, P, Q, T–V, Z	▓ Computation P, R, T, V, X–Z	🕐 Time H, J	◇ Geometry A, B
$\frac{5}{\times 7}$ Math Facts C, G, K, O, S, W	$ Money I, J, X	⚖ Measurement A, B, R	◪ Data D

The *Daily Practice and Problems and Home Practice Guide* in the *Teacher Implementation Guide* includes information on how and when to use the DPP.

Review and Assessment of the Math Facts

By the end of fourth grade, students in *Math Trailblazers* are expected to demonstrate fluency with all the facts. The DPP for this unit continues the systematic, strategies-based approach to reviewing the multiplication and division facts. This unit reviews all five groups of facts—the 5s and 10s, the 2s and 3s, the squares, the 9s, and the last six facts (4×6, 4×7, 4×8, 6×7, 6×8, and 7×8). See items C, G, K, O, S, and W. Note: Part 1 of the Home Practice in the *Discovery*

Assignment Book reminds students to take home their flash cards to practice the facts with a family member. Each group of facts flash cards was distributed in the *Discovery Assignment Book* following the Home Practice in Units 2–6. Blackline masters of all the flash cards, organized by group, are in the *Grade 5 Facts Resource Guide*.

For more information about the distribution and assessment of the math facts, see the TIMS Tutor: *Math Facts* in the *Teacher Implementation Guide* and the *Grade 5 Facts Resource Guide*. Also refer to Unit 2 Lesson Guide 2 and the DPP guide in the *Unit Resource Guide* for Unit 2.

Unit 7 Daily Practice and Problems

Students may solve the items individually, in groups, or as a class. The items may also be assigned for homework. The DPPs are also available on the Teacher Resource CD.

Student Questions	Teacher Notes

A Mystery Angles

Find the missing angle measurements.
Do not use a protractor.

1.
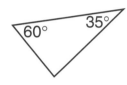

2.
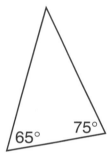

3. The two missing angles have the same measurement.

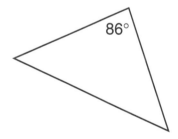

TIMS Bit

1. 85°

2. 40°

3. Each of the two missing angle measurements is 47°.

B Triangles

1. Use a protractor to draw a triangle with one angle measuring 35°. Make one of the other two angles obtuse.

2. Draw a second triangle with one angle measuring 35°. Make the other two angles acute.

TIMS Task

Answers will vary.
Examples are shown below:

1.
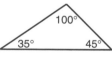

2.

Reviewing the Facts

Solve the given fact. Then name the other related fact or facts in the same fact family.

A. $5 \times 6 =$

B. $7 \times 4 =$

C. $24 \div 8 =$

D. $4 \times 10 =$

E. $81 \div 9 =$

F. $14 \div 7 =$

TIMS Bit

In the next unit, you will test students on all five groups of facts—the 2s and 3s, 5s and 10s, 9s, square numbers, and the last six facts (4×6, 4×7, 4×8, 6×7, 6×8, and 7×8).

A. 30; $6 \times 5 = 30$;
   $30 \div 5 = 6$;
   $30 \div 6 = 5$

B. 28; $4 \times 7 = 28$;
   $28 \div 4 = 7$;
   $28 \div 7 = 4$

C. 3; $24 \div 3 = 8$;
   $8 \times 3 = 24$;
   $3 \times 8 = 24$

D. 40; $10 \times 4 = 40$;
   $40 \div 4 = 10$;
   $40 \div 10 = 4$

E. 9; $9 \times 9 = 81$

F. 2; $14 \div 2 = 7$;
   $7 \times 2 = 14$;
   $2 \times 7 = 14$

At some point during this unit, have student pairs review all the multiplication and division facts using the *Triangle Flash Cards*. Ask them to sort the cards into three piles: those facts they know and can answer quickly, those they can figure out with a strategy, and those they need to learn. Have students update their *Multiplication* and *Division Facts I Know* charts.

D Which Costs More?

Irma made this graph. It shows the number of pounds of fruit and their total cost. It compares the cost of plums to the cost of grapes.

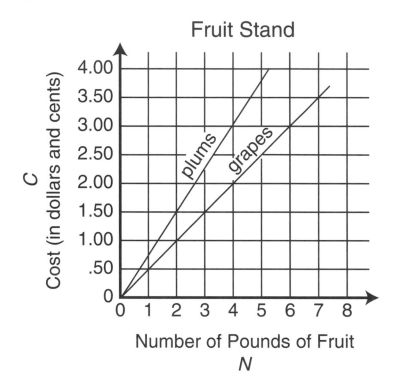

Fruit Stand

1. Which fruit costs more per pound? How do you know?

2. Find the cost of 4 pounds of plums.

3. How many pounds of grapes cost $1.50?

4. Find the cost of 10 pounds of grapes.

TIMS Task

1. plums; the cost of 2 pounds of plums is $1.50 whereas the cost of 2 pounds of grapes is only $1.00. The line for plums is always above the line for grapes.

2. $3.00

3. 3 pounds

4. 1 pound of grapes is $.50 so 10 pounds of grapes are $5.00.

For homework, have students look in their grocery store or in food ads. Ask them to find the cost per pound of a fruit such as apples or bananas. Then have them add the data for their fruit to the graph. How does the cost compare to the cost of plums and grapes in the graph?

Student Questions	Teacher Notes

 E **Greater Than, Less Than, or Equal To**

Replace the *n* to make each sentence true.

A. $\frac{2}{3} = \frac{n}{6}$ B. $\frac{1}{3} < \frac{n}{3}$

C. $50\% = \frac{n}{10}$ D. $50\% < \frac{n}{4}$

E. $2\frac{2}{3} > 2\frac{2}{n}$ F. $20\% < \frac{n}{100}$

TIMS Bit

A. $\frac{2}{3} = \frac{4}{6}$

B. Answers will vary.

$\frac{1}{3} < \frac{2}{3}$

C. $50\% = \frac{5}{10}$

D. Answers will vary.

$50\% < \frac{3}{4}$

E. Answers will vary.

$2\frac{2}{3} > 2\frac{2}{4}$

F. Answers will vary.

$20\% < \frac{25}{100}$

 F *Digits Game*

Draw boxes like these on your paper.

$$\square\square.\square\square\square$$

As your teacher or classmate chooses digits from a deck of digit cards, place them in the boxes. Try to make the largest number. Remember that each digit will be read only once. Once you place a digit, it cannot be moved.

TIMS Task

To begin the game, students draw the set of boxes on their paper. The teacher chooses a digit at random from a set of *Digit Cards (0–9)*. As an alternative, use a deck of playing cards. The ace can stand for 1 and the joker or a face card can stand for zero.) Students place the digits in a box as they try to get the largest number. Once a digit is placed, it cannot be moved. Then the teacher chooses a second digit without replacing the first in the deck. Play continues until the teacher has read enough digits to fill the boxes. The player with the largest number wins. Play again; however, this time students try to make the smallest number.

Student Questions	Teacher Notes

 Reviewing the Facts

Solve the given fact. Then name the other related fact or facts in the same fact family.

A. $8 \times 6 =$

B. $12 \div 4 =$

C. $80 \div 8 =$

D. $40 \div 8 =$

E. $7 \times 9 =$

F. $2 \times 4 =$

TIMS Bit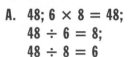

A. 48; $6 \times 8 = 48$;
  $48 \div 6 = 8$;
  $48 \div 8 = 6$

B. 3; $12 \div 3 = 4$;
  $3 \times 4 = 12$;
  $4 \times 3 = 12$

C. 10; $80 \div 10 = 8$;
  $10 \times 8 = 80$;
  $8 \times 10 = 80$

D. 5; $40 \div 5 = 8$;
  $5 \times 8 = 40$;
  $8 \times 5 = 40$

E. 63; $9 \times 7 = 63$;
  $63 \div 7 = 9$;
  $63 \div 9 = 7$

F. 8; $4 \times 2 = 8$;
  $8 \div 2 = 4$;
  $8 \div 4 = 2$

H **Movie Schedules**

The first showing of a new comedy is at 1:20 in the afternoon. The movie is 2 hours and 15 minutes long. There is a twenty minute break between movies. There are four showings of the movie. List the starting and ending times of the four showings.

TIMS Task

1. 1:20 to 3:35

2. 3:55 to 6:10

3. 6:30 to 8:45

4. 9:05 to 11:20

Student Questions	Teacher Notes

 Skip Counting

1. Skip count by dimes to $2.00. Start like this: $0.10, $0.20, $0.30 . . .

2. Skip count by tenths to 2. Start like this: 0.1, 0.2, 0.3 . . .

3. Skip count by quarters to $5.00. Start like this: $0.25, $0.50, $0.75 . . .

4. Skip count by 0.25 (twenty-five hundredths) to 5. Start like this: 0.25, 0.50, 0.75 . . .

TIMS Bit

Skip count in unison as a class. Be sure students say the numbers accurately. For Question 1, for example, they should begin, "10 cents, 20 cents, . . ." For Question 2, they should begin, "one-tenth, two-tenths, . . ." For Question 4, point out to students that they can count two ways: "25 hundredths, 50 hundredths, . . ." or "25 hundredths, 5 tenths, 75 hundredths, 1 . . ."

 Time Is Money

It is 1:50 P.M. when Nila's mother parks the car near Nila's ballet lesson. The parking meter takes 25 cents for each 15 minutes. It only takes quarters. Nila's mother has $1.75 in quarters.

1. If she uses all her quarters, what time will she need to return to her car?

2. If she wants to stay until 4:30, how much more money will she need?

TIMS Task

Have students share the strategies they used to solve the challenge. Possible strategies include:

1. $1.75 ÷ .25 = 7 quarters; 7 × 15 minutes = 1 hour 45 minutes; 1 hr 45 min after 1:50 is 3:35.

2. 3:35 to 4:30 is 55 minutes; 55 minutes is about 4 more intervals of 15 minutes, so she will need 4 more quarters or $1.00.

Reviewing the Facts

Solve the given fact. Then name the other related fact or facts in the same fact family.

A. $10 \times 6 =$

B. $56 \div 7 =$

C. $45 \div 5 =$

D. $6 \times 2 =$

E. $18 \div 3 =$

F. $8 \times 4 =$

TIMS Bit

A. 60; $6 \times 10 = 60$;
   $60 \div 10 = 6$;
   $60 \div 6 = 10$

B. 8; $56 \div 8 = 7$;
   $7 \times 8 = 56$;
   $8 \times 7 = 56$

C. 9; $45 \div 9 = 5$;
   $5 \times 9 = 45$;
   $9 \times 5 = 45$

D. 12; $2 \times 6 = 12$;
   $12 \div 6 = 2$;
   $12 \div 2 = 6$

E. 6; $18 \div 6 = 3$;
   $6 \times 3 = 18$;
   $3 \times 6 = 18$

F. 32; $4 \times 8 = 32$;
   $32 \div 4 = 8$;
   $32 \div 8 = 4$

Have students update their *Multiplication* and *Division Facts I Know* charts. Remind students to take home their *Triangle Flash Cards* to review the facts they have yet to circle on their charts. The Home Practice for this unit reminds students to take home their flash cards.

Student Questions	Teacher Notes

 Using the Centiwheel

Use your centiwheel to complete the following:

1. Name a fraction that is close to 0. Give it as a common fraction, decimal, and percent.

2. Name a fraction that is just a little less than $\frac{1}{4}$. Give it as a common fraction, decimal, and percent.

3. Name a fraction that is just a little more than $\frac{1}{2}$. Give it as a common fraction, decimal, and percent.

4. Name a fraction that is close to 1. Give it as a common fraction, decimal, and percent.

TIMS Task

Answers will vary.
Examples follow:

1. $\frac{2}{100}$; .02; 2%

2. $\frac{23}{100}$; .23; 23%

3. $\frac{52}{100}$; .52; 52%

4. $\frac{98}{100}$; .98; 98%

 Ordering Decimals

Put the following sets of numbers in order from smallest to largest.

A. $2\frac{3}{4}$, 2.5, 2.0, 0.2

B. 4.5, $4\frac{1}{4}$, 0.4, $4\frac{1}{5}$, 4

C. 71, 7.1, 710, 0.7, 710.1, $71\frac{1}{2}$

TIMS Bit

A. 0.2, 2.0, 2.5, $2\frac{3}{4}$

B. 0.4, 4, $4\frac{1}{5}$, $4\frac{1}{4}$, 4.5

C. 0.7, 7.1, 71, $71\frac{1}{2}$, 710, 710.1

 The Important Point

Place a decimal point in the following numbers so the four numbers will increase in order from left to right. Read the numbers to a friend.

30274   30269   29145   14058

Try to do this in more than one way.

TIMS Challenge

Answers will vary.
Examples:

.30274	30.274
3.0269	302.69
29.145	2914.5
140.58	14058.

Student Questions	Teacher Notes

 Reviewing the Facts

Solve the given fact. Then name the other related fact or facts in the same fact family.

A. $24 \div 4 =$ B. $5 \times 5 =$

C. $70 \div 10 =$ D. $18 \div 9 =$

E. $7 \times 6 =$ F. $15 \div 3 =$

TIMS Bit

A. 6; $24 \div 6 = 4$;
    $6 \times 4 = 24$;
    $4 \times 6 = 24$

B. 25; $25 \div 5 = 5$

C. 7; $70 \div 7 = 10$;
    $10 \times 7 = 70$;
    $7 \times 10 = 70$

D. 2; $18 \div 2 = 9$;
    $2 \times 9 = 18$;
    $9 \times 2 = 18$

E. 42; $6 \times 7 = 42$;
    $42 \div 6 = 7$;
    $42 \div 7 = 6$

F. 5; $15 \div 5 = 3$;
    $5 \times 3 = 15$;
    $3 \times 5 = 15$

P **Sums and Differences**

Estimate to answer the following. Do not use paper and pencil.

1. Is $3.694 + 4.076$ closer to 7 or 8? How do you know?

2. Is $5 - 3.7$ more or less than 2? How do you know?

3. Is $1.355 + 9.207$ more or less than 10.5? How do you know?

4. Is $14.342 - 0.018$ more or less than 14? How do you know?

5. Is $13.9 + 1.012$ more or less than 15? How do you know?

TIMS Task

1. 8

2. less than 2

3. more than 10.5

4. more than 14

5. less than 15

Student Questions	**Teacher Notes**

 Decimals

Write a decimal:

1. between 5 and 6

2. between 1 and 2

3. just a little bigger than 3

4. just a little less than 9

5. between $\frac{1}{2}$ and .9

6. between 6.5 and 7

TIMS Bit

Answers will vary.
Examples follow:

1. 5.5

2. 1.3

3. 3.1; 3.01

4. 8.9; 8.99

5. .8

6. 6.8

Adding Lengths

1. A.   Draw a line segment that is 4.6 cm long. Label it $\overline{CD}$.

   B.   Draw line segment $\overline{DE}$ to the right of $\overline{CD}$ that is 3.7 cm.

   C.   Measure from C to E. Does $\overline{CE}$ measure 4.6 cm + 3.7 cm?

2. Model 6.2 + 4.9 by drawing two line segments $\overline{RS}$ and $\overline{ST}$.

3. Add 6.2 + 4.9. Measure your line segment ($\overline{RT}$). Does $\overline{RT}$ measure 6.2 cm + 4.9 cm?

TIMS Task

1. C ——4.6 cm—— D ——3.7 cm—— E   **yes**

2. R ——6.2 cm—— S ——4.9 cm—— T

3. 11.1 cm

Student Questions	Teacher Notes

 Reviewing the Facts

Solve the given fact. Then name the other related fact or facts in the same fact family.

A. $6 \div 3 =$

B. $8 \times 8 =$

C. $35 \div 7 =$

D. $20 \div 5 =$

E. $9 \times 6 =$

F. $27 \div 9 =$

TIMS Bit

A. 2; $6 \div 2 = 3$;
$2 \times 3 = 6$;
$3 \times 2 = 6$

B. 64; $64 \div 8 = 8$

C. 5; $35 \div 5 = 7$;
$5 \times 7 = 35$;
$7 \times 5 = 35$

D. 4; $20 \div 4 = 5$;
$5 \times 4 = 20$;
$4 \times 5 = 20$

E. 54; $6 \times 9 = 54$;
$54 \div 6 = 9$;
$54 \div 9 = 6$

F. 3; $27 \div 3 = 9$;
$9 \times 3 = 27$;
$3 \times 9 = 27$

T **Practice**

Solve the following using paper and pencil. Estimate to be sure your answers are reasonable.

A. $34 + 78 =$

B. $582 - 465 =$

C. $2708 \times 6 =$

D. $89 \times 12 =$

E. $2649 \div 6 =$

F. $5893 + 3075 =$

TIMS Task

A. 112

B. 117

C. 16,248

D. 1068

E. 441 R3

F. 8968

Student Questions	Teacher Notes

 Missing Decimal Points

Professor Peabody forgot to put decimal points in the numbers below. He does know that the "6" in each number stands for six-tenths.

Put a decimal point in each number so the 6 stands for six-tenths. Now say the numbers aloud to a partner.

A. 1360   B. 1206   C. 603

D. 126   E. 367   F. 1634

TIMS Bit

A. 13.60
B. 120.6
C. .603
D. 12.6
E. 3.67
F. 1.634

 Multiplying Decimals

Estimate the products. Then solve each problem using paper and pencil.

A. $3.4 \times 2.1 =$ B. $5.6 \times 10.4 =$

C. $8.2 \times 8.9 =$ D. $0.89 \times .95 =$

E. $18 \times .96 =$ F. $28.85 \times 4 =$

TIMS Task

Estimates will vary. One reasonable estimate is listed for each.

A. 6; 7.14
B. 60; 58.24
C. 72; 72.98
D. just less than 1; 0.8455
E. just less than 18; 17.28
F. 120; 115.4

 Reviewing the Facts

Solve the given fact. Then name the other related fact or facts in the same fact family.

A. $7 \times 3 =$ B. $36 \div 6 =$

C. $72 \div 8 =$ D. $4 \times 9 =$

E. $50 \div 5 =$ F. $7 \times 7 =$

TIMS Bit

A. 21; $3 \times 7 = 21$;
   $21 \div 3 = 7$;
   $21 \div 7 = 3$
B. 6; $6 \times 6 = 36$
C. 9; $72 \div 9 = 8$;
   $8 \times 9 = 72$;
   $9 \times 8 = 72$
D. 36; $9 \times 4 = 36$;
   $36 \div 4 = 9$;
   $36 \div 9 = 4$
E. 10; $50 \div 10 = 5$;
   $10 \times 5 = 50$;
   $5 \times 10 = 50$
F. 49; $49 \div 7 = 7$

Rich in Pounds

Four quarters (25¢) weigh 0.05 pound. You need 7200 quarters to equal the average weight of a 12-year-old.

1. What is the average weight of a 12-year-old?

2. How much do 7200 quarters equal in dollars and cents?

TIMS Challenge

Solution strategies will vary.

1. 90 pounds

2. $7200 \div 4 = \$1800$

 Adding and Subtracting Fractions

A. $\frac{3}{5} + \frac{3}{10} =$ B. $\frac{7}{8} - \frac{1}{2} =$

C. $\frac{1}{6} + \frac{1}{3} =$ D. $\frac{1}{2} - \frac{1}{3} =$

TIMS Bit

A. $\frac{9}{10}$

B. $\frac{3}{8}$

C. $\frac{3}{6}$ or $\frac{1}{2}$

D. $\frac{1}{6}$

 Practice

Solve the following using paper and pencil. Estimate to be sure your answers are reasonable.

A. $836 + 47 =$ B. $2058 - 1467 =$

C. $66 \times 33 =$ D. $7399 \div 8 =$

E. $4702 \div 7 =$ F. $3967 - 1098 =$

TIMS Task

A. 883

B. 591

C. 2178

D. 924 R7

E. 671 R5

F. 2869

Lesson 1

Fractions, Decimals, and Percents

Lesson Overview

Estimated Class Sessions
2-3

Students use an interlocking centiwheel model to investigate the idea that fractions, decimals, and percents can be different symbolic representations of the same quantity.

Key Content

- Translating between different representations of decimals, (concrete, pictorial, and symbolic).
- Using fractions, decimals, and percents to represent the same quantity.

Key Vocabulary

- centiwheel
- decimal
- fraction
- percent

Math Facts

DPP item C reviews math facts.

Homework

1. Students complete homework *Questions 1–5* in the *Student Guide*.
2. Students complete the *Designing Quilts* Homework Page in the *Discovery Assignment Book*. They will use their quilt designs in Lesson 2.
3. Assign Parts 1 and 2 of the Home Practice in the *Discovery Assignment Book*.

Assessment

Use Part 3 of the Home Practice as a quiz.

Curriculum Sequence

Before This Unit

Fractions

In Grade 5 Unit 3 Lesson 3 students investigated equivalent fractions using pattern blocks and number lines. Given a fraction, they wrote equivalent fractions with different denominators. In Unit 3 Lesson 4 they used these models to compare fractions. In Unit 5 students used pattern blocks, geoboards, and dot paper to model fractions. In Unit 5 Lesson 4 students compared fractions with unlike denominators by rewriting the fractions with common denominators. In Unit 5 Lessons 6 and 7 students began adding and subtracting fractions.

Decimals and Percents

In Grade 3 Unit 15 and Grade 4 Unit 10 students used base-ten pieces to model and compare decimals.

After This Unit

Fractions

Students change fractions to percents in their analysis of data in Unit 8 Lesson 5 *Life Spans* and in the experiment in Unit 8 Lesson 6 *Comparing Lives of Animals and Soap Bubbles*.

Decimals

Students will continue changing fractions to decimals in Units 8 and 9. In their work in the lab *Circumference vs. Diameter* in Unit 14, students work with terminating and repeating decimals as well as π, an irrational number.

Materials List

Supplies and Copies

Student	Teacher
Supplies for Each Student	**Supplies**
• scissors	
• hole punch, optional	
Supplies for Each Student Pair	
• 1 set of base-ten pieces (2 flats, 20 skinnies, 15 bits), optional	
Copies	**Copies/Transparencies**
• 1 copy of *Tenths and Hundredths* per student, optional (*Unit Resource Guide* Pages 42–47)	• 1 copy of *Centiwheel Disks,* 1 enlarged disk on white paper and 1 enlarged disk on colored paper for demonstration, optional (*Unit Resource Guide* Page 48)
• 1 copy of *Centiwheel Disks* per student, 1 disk on colored paper and 1 disk on white paper (*Unit Resource Guide* Page 48)	
• 1 small disk from *Small Centiwheels* per student (*Unit Resource Guide* Page 49)	
• 2 copies of *Three-trial Data Table* per student (*Unit Resource Guide* Page 50)	

All blackline masters including assessment, transparency, and DPP masters are also on the Teacher Resource CD.

Student Books
Fractions, Decimals, and Percents (*Student Guide* Pages 222–229)
Designing Quilts (*Discovery Assignment Book* Page 101)

Daily Practice and Problems and Home Practice
DPP items A–D (*Unit Resource Guide* Pages 16–18)
Home Practice Parts 1–3 (*Discovery Assignment Book* Pages 97–98)

Note: Classrooms whose pacing differs significantly from the suggested pacing of the units should use the Math Facts Calendar in Section 4 of the *Facts Resource Guide* to ensure students receive the complete math facts program.

Daily Practice and Problems

Suggestions for using the DPPs are on page 39.

A. Bit: Mystery Angles (URG p. 16)

Find the missing angle measurements.
Do not use a protractor.

1.   2.

3. The two missing angles have the same
   measurement.

B. Task: Triangles (URG p. 16)

1. Use a protractor to draw a triangle with
   one angle measuring 35°. Make one of the other
   two angles obtuse.
2. Draw a second triangle with one angle measuring 35°. Make the other two angles acute.

C. Bit: Reviewing the Facts (URG p. 17)

Solve the given fact. Then name the other
related fact or facts in the same fact family.

A. $5 \times 6 =$ B. $7 \times 4 =$

C. $24 \div 8 =$ D. $4 \times 10 =$

E. $81 \div 9 =$ F. $14 \div 7 =$

D. Task: Which Costs More? (URG p. 18)

Irma made this graph. It shows the number of
pounds of fruit and their total cost. It compares the
cost of plums to the cost of grapes.

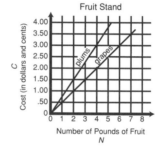

1. Which fruit costs more per pound?
   How do you know?

2. Find the cost of 4 pounds of plums.

3. How many pounds of grapes cost $1.50?

4. Find the cost of 10 pounds of grapes.

Make copies of the *Centiwheel Disks* Activity Page in the *Unit Resource Guide.* Use colored paper for half the copies. Pair students so they share a white-paper copy and a colored-paper copy. Each student needs one white disk and one colored disk. Model the process of precisely cutting along the radius and slipping the wheels together to make an interlocking **centiwheel** as shown in Figure 6.

Make copies of the *Small Centiwheels* Activity Page in the *Unit Resource Guide* and laminate them if possible.

Make a large centiwheel for demonstration purposes. Copy one centiwheel on the *Centiwheel Disks* Activity Page in the *Unit Resource Guide* on white paper, increasing the wheel's size as large as possible. Make a second colored centiwheel of the same size.

Teaching the Activity

Part 1 **A Review: Tenths and Hundredths (optional)**

For students with little experience with decimals, begin the lesson using the *Tenths and Hundredths* Activity Pages in the *Unit Resource Guide.* These optional pages use activities from third and fourth grades to introduce tenths and hundredths using base-ten pieces. For these pages, a flat represents one whole, a skinny represents one-tenth, and a bit represents one-hundredth.

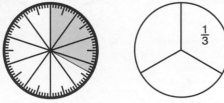

1 whole $\frac{1}{10} = 0.1$ $\frac{1}{100} = 0.01$

Figure 5: *A flat is one whole, a skinny represents one-tenth, and a bit represents one-hundredth.*

Content Note

Centiwheels. In this lesson, we explore the relationship of a fraction to the whole using two centiwheels of different colors. They are cut along a radius and slipped together to make an interlocking **centiwheel** as shown in Figure 6. Any part less than the whole can simultaneously model a fraction, decimal, or percent since each centiwheel is marked with 100 equal intervals around the edge. See Figure 6. The area of the centiwheel is defined as one whole.

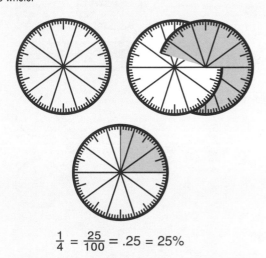

$\frac{1}{4} = \frac{25}{100} = .25 = 25\%$

Figure 6: *Interlocking centiwheel disks*

Note that not all fractions translate exactly to decimals using this model. For instance, we cannot model $\frac{1}{3}$ exactly using this model since $\frac{1}{3}$ of 100 is not a whole number. However, we can approximate $\frac{1}{3}$ using the centiwheel: $\frac{33}{100}$ or 0.33 is close to $\frac{1}{3}$. (Fractions such as $\frac{1}{3}$ will be further investigated in Unit 9.) See Figure 7.

Figure 7: $\frac{33}{100}$ *is close to* $\frac{1}{3}$

TIMS Tip

Save the large and small centiwheels for use in Units 8, 9, and 14.

The *Fractions, Decimals, and Percents* Activity Pages in the *Student Guide* introduce students to the centiwheel and show how to construct one. After students make their centiwheels, have them determine the number of intervals (100) around the edge of the centiwheel *(Questions 1–2).* Introduce the idea that each small section represents one-hundredth of the whole (the circle).

Ask students to look at the centiwheel that models $\frac{1}{4}$ in the *Student Guide.* Using the example as a guide, ask students to model $\frac{1}{4}$ with their own centiwheels. The example in the *Student Guide* shows how to use the centiwheel to model a fraction and find an equivalent fraction with a denominator of 100. Discuss the fact that since 25 sections out of 100 are colored, the fraction $\frac{1}{4}$ is equivalent to $\frac{25}{100}$. This example should help students read the centiwheel. Use the following prompts if they need more explanation. These prompts emphasize the three different lengths of lines that appear on the centiwheel.

- *Look at the long lines that run through the centiwheel. How many equal sections do they divide the wheel into?* (10)

- *Look at the shortest lines. They divide each of the 10 sections into smaller intervals. How many equal intervals are there in each of the 10 sections?* (10)

- *How many of these small intervals run along the entire edge of the wheel?* (100)

- *Look at the medium lines. How do they divide each of the 10 sections?* (They divide each section in half. So there are five intervals to the left of each medium line and five intervals to the right.)

- *How did the long and medium lines help Edward read the centiwheel?* (He didn't have to count by 1s. He first counted by 10s. Then the medium line told him right away that he had 5 hundredths more.)

- *Model $\frac{37}{100}$ on your centiwheel. Describe how to show $\frac{37}{100}$.* (First I use the long lines as my guide. I turn the wheel to show three of the large shaded areas. This shows 10, 20, 30 hundredths. Then, I turn it to the next medium line to reach 35 hundredths. Then, I use the small lines. I need to turn it 2 more little spaces or 2 more hundredths.)

TIMS Tip

Remind students that the centiwheel is made up of 100 intervals. These intervals are *not* degrees, since 360° form a circle.

Question 3 reminds students that they know another strategy for finding equivalent fractions: $\frac{1}{4} = \frac{1 \times 25}{4 \times 25} = \frac{25}{100}$. *Questions 4–5* ask students to model $\frac{1}{2}$ and $\frac{3}{4}$ on the centiwheels. By determining the number of intervals within the shaded fractional part, students concretely experience that 50 intervals out of 100 make up $\frac{1}{2}$ of the centiwheel and 75 intervals out of 100 make up $\frac{3}{4}$ of the centiwheel. We can translate the fraction $\frac{1}{2}$ to $\frac{50}{100}$ and the fraction $\frac{3}{4}$ to $\frac{75}{100}$. Stress that both fractions $\frac{1}{2}$ and $\frac{50}{100}$ represent the same relationship or quantity. Likewise, $\frac{3}{4}$ and $\frac{75}{100}$ represent the same relationship or quantity. See Figure 8.

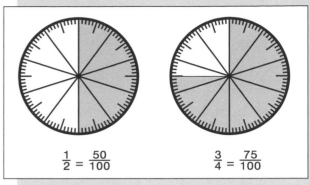

$$\frac{1}{2} = \frac{50}{100} \qquad \frac{3}{4} = \frac{75}{100}$$

Figure 8: *Using the centiwheel to model $\frac{1}{2}$ and $\frac{3}{4}$*

Part 3 Translations

The Translations section in the *Student Guide* returns to the fraction $\frac{1}{4}$. Have students model the fraction $\frac{1}{4}$ on their interlocking centiwheels. Again, have them determine the number of intervals within the fractional part (25). Read the text along with your students. Using the centiwheel, $\frac{1}{4}$ or $\frac{25}{100}$ is rewritten as 0.25 and then translated to 25%.

Emphasize that percent is not a new idea, but just another way to write and express decimals and fractions. Discuss with students that **percent** means "per 100." You can again connect this idea to the unit of one dollar, since there are 100 cents in a dollar. Therefore, the decimal .25 is the same as 25%. The quarter has a value of 25% of a dollar.

> **Content Note**
>
> **Dollars and Cents.** Twenty-five cents written as part of one dollar is $0.25 or $.25. Written as a decimal $.25 means twenty-five hundredths of one dollar; .25¢ is **not** 25 cents. The symbols .25¢ mean twenty-five hundredths of one cent or $\frac{1}{4}$ of a cent.

Questions 6–7 ask students to write $\frac{1}{2}$ and $\frac{3}{4}$ as decimals and percents. Encourage students to model the fractions $\frac{1}{2}$ and $\frac{3}{4}$ using the centiwheel so they concretely see the relationship between the fraction, decimal, and percent (e.g., $\frac{1}{2}$ or $\frac{50}{100}$, 0.50, and 50%). Also, relate $\frac{1}{2}$ and $\frac{3}{4}$ to money, namely $\frac{1}{2}$ of a dollar or $.50 and three quarters or $.75. Relate the translations of $\frac{50}{100}$ to 50% and $\frac{75}{100}$ to 75% to money as well. $.50 is 50% of a dollar. $.75 is 75% of a dollar.

> **Content Note**
>
> **Fractions and Decimals.** A **fraction** is a number that can be written as $\frac{a}{b}$ where a and b are whole numbers and b is not zero. Using this definition both $\frac{5}{10}$ and 0.5 are fractions because they both can be written as $\frac{5}{10}$. We call $\frac{5}{10}$ a **common fraction** and we call 0.5 a **decimal fraction**. The terms **common fraction** and **decimal fraction** are used in the *Student Guide* to emphasize that both notations can represent the same quantity. However, we usually refer to common fractions as just "fractions" and decimal fractions as just "decimals."

> **TIMS Tip**
>
> Use money to make a connection between fractions and the conventional form for writing decimals. Review with students that there are four quarters in a dollar and each quarter represents $\frac{1}{4}$ of the whole (the dollar = 100 cents). Students already know how 25¢ is written as a part of one dollar ($.25). We can write .25 to represent $\frac{1}{4}$ of a unit that is partitioned into 100 pieces. The decimal 0.25 represents $\frac{1}{4}$ of one whole unit.

Student Guide - page 224 (Answers on p. 52)

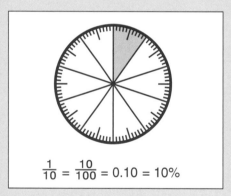

$$\frac{1}{10} = \frac{10}{100} = 0.10 = 10\%$$

Figure 9: *Using the centiwheel to model $\frac{10}{100}$*

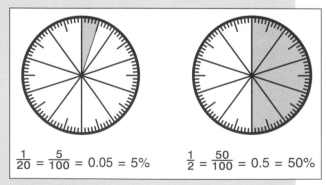

$$\frac{1}{20} = \frac{5}{100} = 0.05 = 5\% \qquad \frac{1}{2} = \frac{50}{100} = 0.5 = 50\%$$

Figure 10: *Using the centiwheel to model $\frac{1}{20}$ and $\frac{1}{2}$*

One-tenth is an important benchmark for comparing and ordering decimals. **Question 8** asks students to use the centiwheel to write one-tenth as a common fraction, decimal fraction, and percent. Since $\frac{1}{10} = \frac{10}{100}$ and $\frac{10}{100} = 0.10$, then $\frac{1}{10} = 0.10 = 10\%$.

Use the centiwheels to help students review different notations for tenths. (More work with equivalent representations for tenths follows in Lessons 2 and 3.) Choose from these discussion prompts:

- *Model one-tenth on your centiwheels. Now as you skip count by tenths, model each tenth you say.* (One-tenth, two-tenths, . . . ten-tenths or one whole)

- *How do we write one-tenth as a common fraction?* ($\frac{1}{10}$)

- *Skip count by tenths using fractions. Count out loud and write the fractions.* ($\frac{1}{10}, \frac{2}{10}, \frac{3}{10}, \ldots \frac{10}{10}$ or 1)

- *How do we write one-tenth as a decimal fraction?* (0.1)

- *Skip count by tenths using decimals. Count out loud as before and write the decimals.* (Have students say, "one-tenth, two-tenths, . . ." as they write "0.1, 0.2, 0.3, . . .1.0")

- *Model one-tenth on your centiwheels. How do you write $\frac{1}{10}$ as a fraction with a denominator of 100?* ($\frac{1}{10} = \frac{10}{100}$)

- *How do you write $\frac{10}{100}$ as a decimal?* (One way to write $\frac{10}{100}$ is 0.10. Another way is 0.1.)

- *Model ten-hundredths on your centiwheels. Skip count by ten-hundredths. Say each fraction out loud.* (Ten-hundredths, twenty-hundredths, thirty-hundredths, . . . one-hundred hundredths or one whole) See Figure 9.

- *Skip count by ten-hundredths using decimals. Count out loud as before and write each decimal.* (Have students say, "ten-hundredths, twenty-hundredths, . . ." as they write "0.10, 0.20, 0.30, . . . 1.00")

- *Model each percent on your centiwheels as you skip count. Begin this way, 10%, 20%, . . .* (10%, 20%, . . . 100%)

Question 9 asks students to write $\frac{1}{20}$ as a fraction, decimal, and percent. Since $\frac{1}{20} = \frac{5}{100}$, and $\frac{5}{100} = 0.05$, then $\frac{1}{20} = 0.05 = 5\%$. Remind students that $\frac{5}{100}$ is written 0.05 as a decimal. To help them discriminate between 0.5 and 0.05, ask them to model 0.5 (or $\frac{1}{2}$) on their centiwheels. Then, ask them to model 0.05 or $\frac{1}{20}$ again. Connect the correct symbols to the corresponding models on the centiwheels. See Figure 10.

Since the visual discrimination of fifths and tenths using the centiwheel is not always easy, do not dwell on these translations. However, we do want students to know they can make these translations. To answer

Question 10, students first model $\frac{1}{5}$ on the centiwheel. Then they write $\frac{1}{5}$ as $\frac{20}{100}$. Finally they write $\frac{20}{100} = 0.20 = 20\%$.

Encourage students to use the interlocking centiwheel to make some of the translations in **Questions 11–14** (e.g., $0.80 = 80\%$; $95\% = \frac{95}{100}$; $0.08 = \frac{8}{100}$). They can make other translations readily without the model. As students are working, be sure they can make distinctions between 7% and 70% and 0.08 and 0.80.

Assign homework **Questions 1–5** after Part 3.

Part 4 **Using the Centiwheel to Compare Fractions**

Next, use the interlocking centiwheel to explore some decimals, fractions, and percents that we cannot translate into familiar fractions. For example, have students model $\frac{29}{100}$ using the centiwheel. Ask:

- *Is the fractional part, shown on the interlocking centiwheel, more or less than $\frac{1}{2}$? More or less than $\frac{1}{4}$?*

Students should work in pairs to answer **Questions 15–17** in the *Student Guide* which ask similar questions.

If students can easily visualize fifths and tenths using the centiwheel, challenge them by using prompts such as the following:

- *Model $\frac{8}{100}$ using the centiwheel. Is $\frac{8}{100}$ closer to $\frac{1}{4}$, $\frac{1}{5}$, or $\frac{1}{10}$?* ($\frac{1}{10}$) (See Figure 11.)

- *Model 39% using the centiwheel. Is 39% closer to $\frac{1}{2}$, $\frac{1}{4}$, or $\frac{2}{5}$?* ($\frac{2}{5}$)

- *Model 0.87 using the centiwheel. Is 0.87 closer to $\frac{3}{4}$, $\frac{4}{5}$, or $\frac{9}{10}$?* ($\frac{9}{10}$)

Part 5 **Using the Small Centiwheel**

Have students turn to the Using the Small Centiwheel section in the *Student Guide.* Distribute one small centiwheel to each student from the *Small Centiwheels* Activity Page in the *Unit Resource Guide.* An example in the *Student Guide* illustrates how to use the small centiwheel to translate fractions on a circle graph to equivalent fractions with denominators of 100 **(Questions 18–19).** See Figure 12.

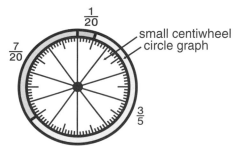

Figure 12: *Using the small centiwheel, we see that:*
$\frac{1}{20} = \frac{5}{100}$, $\frac{7}{20} = \frac{35}{100}$, and $\frac{3}{5} = \frac{60}{100}$.

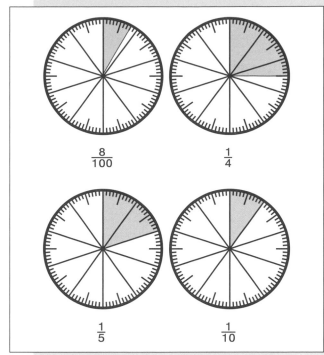

Figure 11: *Is $\frac{8}{100}$ closer to $\frac{1}{4}$, $\frac{1}{5}$, or $\frac{1}{10}$?*

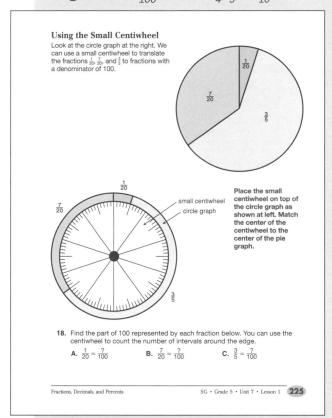

Using the Small Centiwheel
Look at the circle graph at the right. We can use a small centiwheel to translate the fractions $\frac{1}{20}$, $\frac{7}{20}$, and $\frac{3}{5}$ to fractions with a denominator of 100.

Place the small centiwheel on top of the circle graph as shown at left. Match the center of the centiwheel to the center of the pie graph.

18. Find the part of 100 represented by each fraction below. You can use the centiwheel to count the number of intervals around the edge.

A. $\frac{1}{20} = \frac{?}{100}$ **B.** $\frac{7}{20} = \frac{?}{100}$ **C.** $\frac{3}{5} = \frac{?}{100}$

Fractions, Decimals, and Percents   SG • Grade 5 • Unit 7 • Lesson 1   **225**

Student Guide - page 225 *(Answers on p. 52)*

TIMS Tip

To use the small centiwheel, place it in the center of the circle graph, making sure that the center of the centiwheel is directly over the center of the circle graph. If your hole punch reaches the center of the small centiwheel, punch a hole in the center.

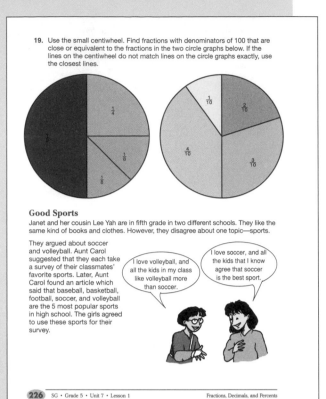

Student Guide - page 226 (Answers on p. 53)

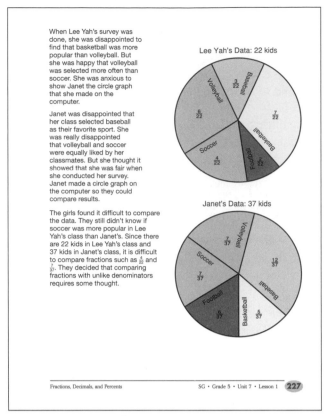

Student Guide - page 227

In the Good Sports section in the *Student Guide,* students apply the translation ideas explored in Part 2. Lee Yah and her cousin Janet have difficulty trying to compare data displayed on circle graphs because the fractions have different denominators. Students use the small centiwheel to translate fractions to equivalent (or approximately equivalent) fractions with a denominator of 100, to decimals, and to percents *(Questions 20–21).* Then they compare the data *(Question 23).* Students will need two copies of a *Three-trial Data Table* to complete *Questions 20–21. Question 22* asks students to total the numbers in the percent column. Students should realize that the decimal representations taken from the centiwheel are not exact, so the total may be slightly different from 100%.

Student Guide - page 228 (Answers on p. 53)

Math Facts

DPP item C reviews the multiplication and division facts using fact families.

Homework and Practice

- After Part 3 of this lesson, have students complete homework *Questions 1–5.*

- Have students complete the data tables and data analysis in *Questions 20–23* in the Good Sports section of the *Student Guide* for homework.

- After students complete the lesson, assign the Quilt Designs Homework section in the *Student Guide* and the *Designing Quilts* Homework Page in the *Discovery Assignment Book.* This homework assignment will be used in Lesson 2.

- Assign DPP items A and B to review angles and triangles. Use item D to practice reading and interpreting graphs.

- Assign Parts 1 and 2 of the Home Practice. Part 1 reminds students to review their facts. Part 2 provides practice with computation of whole numbers.

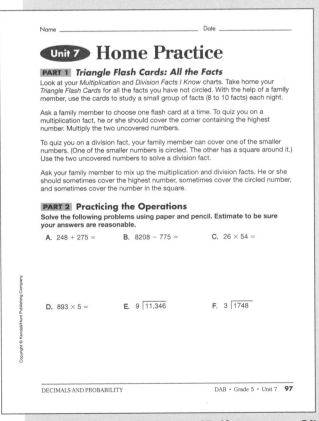

Student Guide - page 229 (Answers on p. 54)

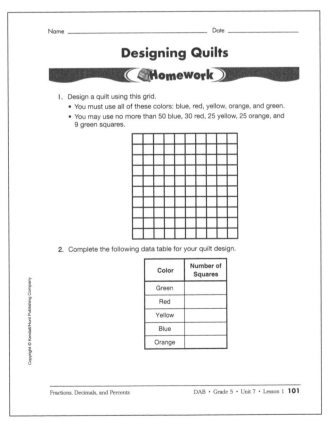

Discovery Assignment Book - page 101 (Answers on p. 55)

Discovery Assignment Book - page 97 (Answers on p. 54)

Discovery Assignment Book - page 98 (Answers on p. 55)

Assessment

Use Part 3 of the Home Practice as a quiz.

Answers for Parts 1–3 of the Home Practice are in the Answer Key at the end of this lesson and at the end of this unit.

Math Facts and Daily Practice and Problems

DPP items A–D review math facts, geometry, and graphing.

Part 1. A Review: Tenths and Hundredths (optional)

Students with little experience with decimals can use the *Tenths and Hundredths* Activity Pages in the *Unit Resource Guide.* These optional pages use activities from Grades 3 and 4 to introduce tenths and hundredths using base-ten pieces.

Part 2. Using the Centiwheel to Name Equivalent Fractions

1. Students make centiwheels using the *Centiwheel Disks* Activity Page in the *Unit Resource Guide.*
2. Use *Questions 1–5* in the *Student Guide* and the discussion prompts in the Lesson Guide to introduce the centiwheel.

Part 3. Translations

1. Discuss percents using the Translations section in the *Student Guide.* Discuss the translation of $\frac{1}{4}$ to $\frac{25}{100}$ to 0.25 and 25%. Connect these fractions to money.
2. Students use centiwheels to translate between fractions, decimals, and percents. *(Questions 6–14)*

Part 4. Using the Centiwheel to Compare Fractions

1. Students use centiwheels to model fractions such as $\frac{43}{100}$ and then identify a benchmark fraction close to the given number such as $\frac{1}{2}$.
2. Students work in pairs to complete *Questions 15–17* in the *Student Guide.*

Part 5. Using the Small Centiwheel

1. Distribute small centiwheels from the *Small Centiwheels* Activity Page in the *Unit Resource Guide* and use *Questions 18–19* to explain how to use them.
2. Students use small centiwheels to complete the Good Sports section of the *Student Guide.* They need two copies of a *Three-trial Data Table* to complete *Questions 20–21.* Students can complete the data tables for homework.

Homework

1. Students complete homework *Questions 1–5* in the *Student Guide.*
2. Students complete the *Designing Quilts* Homework Page in the *Discovery Assignment Book.* They will use their quilt designs in Lesson 2.
3. Assign Parts 1 and 2 of the Home Practice in the *Discovery Assignment Book.*

Assessment

Use Part 3 of the Home Practice as a quiz.

Answer Key is on pages 51–58.

Notes:

Tenths and Hundredths

A New Rule for Base-Ten Pieces

Doing mathematics is sometimes like playing a game. Just as you cannot play a game without rules, you cannot do mathematics without rules. But, just as people sometimes change game rules, we sometimes change rules in mathematics. And, just as we can still play a game if everyone agrees to the new rules, we can still do mathematics if everyone agrees to the new rules.

Now we are going to change a rule for base-ten pieces. When you worked with base-ten pieces before, usually a bit was one whole. When a bit is the unit, then a skinny is 10 units and a flat is 100 units. Now we are going to change which piece is the whole. **For now, a flat will be one whole.**

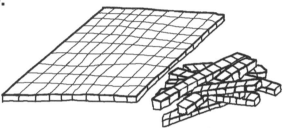

1. Use skinnies to cover a flat.

   A. How many skinnies did you use?

   B. If a flat is 1 whole, then what fraction is a skinny?

One-tenth is a fraction that can be written as 0.1 or $\frac{1}{10}$. Fractions like $\frac{1}{10}$ are called "common fractions" or just "fractions." Fractions like 0.1 are called "decimal fractions" or just "decimals." The decimal point tells us that the numbers to the right of the decimal point are smaller than 1.

$$\frac{1 \leftarrow \text{numerator}}{10 \leftarrow \text{denominator}} \qquad 0.1$$

$$\uparrow$$
$$\text{decimal point}$$

2. **A.** Place 7 skinnies on your flat. Skip count by tenths as you place each skinny. Start like this: one-tenth, two-tenths, three-tenths. . . .

   B. What fraction of the flat is 7 skinnies?

   C. Write this fraction as a common fraction and a decimal fraction.

3. **A.** Put 5 skinnies on your flat. Skip count by tenths as you place each skinny.

   B. Write this number as a fraction. What is another name for this fraction?

   C. Write this number as a decimal.

     Blackline Master

Name _____ Date _____

Tenths Helper Chart

You can use the Tenths Helper Chart to show how many tenths are in 1 and 2 wholes.

4. **A.** Cover your Tenths Helper Chart with flats. How many flats did you use?

   B. What number does this represent?

5. **A.** Place 10 skinnies on your Tenths Helper Chart. Count by tenths as you place each skinny on the chart.

   B. When you skip count by tenths what number comes after 9 tenths? (*Hint:* There is more than one way to answer this question.)

6. Linda knows that 10 skinnies cover one whole. She recorded this 3 ways: 1, 1.0, and $\frac{10}{10}$. Explain how each of these represents the same number. (*Hint:* What does the zero mean in 1.0? What do the numerator and denominator tell you in $\frac{10}{10}$?)

7. **A.** Continue placing skinnies on your Tenths Helper Chart. What number will you say as you place the eleventh skinny on the chart? (*Hint:* There is more than one answer to this question.)

   B. How many skinnies does it take to cover the Tenths Helper Chart?

   C. How many tenths are in two wholes?

Keenya uses a Tenths Helper Chart to show tenths. First she places 12 skinnies on the chart. She counts by tenths as she places each skinny. Then she records the value of 12 skinnies on the chart on the twelfth row as a decimal (1.2), as a fraction ($\frac{12}{10}$), and as a mixed number ($1\frac{2}{10}$).

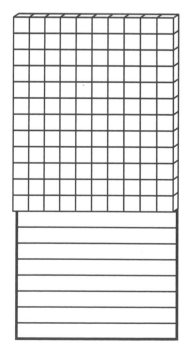

First place 12 skinnies on your chart.

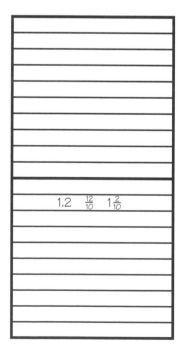

Then, record the value in more than one way.

Blackline Master

Use the Tenths Helper Chart to complete Questions 8–9. Use the skinnies to show each number, then record its value on the chart as a decimal, a fraction, and a mixed number.

8. **A.** 17 skinnies   **B.** 4 skinnies   **C.** 15 skinnies

9. Fill in all of the values in your Tenths Helper Chart. If needed, use skinnies to build each number.

Hundredths

Jackie is counting the pennies in her penny bank to see how many dollars she has. She puts the pennies into piles of 100 since she knows that 100 pennies equal 1 dollar. Jackie knows that 1 penny is one-hundredth of a dollar. You can write the fraction for one-hundredth as a common fraction or as a decimal fraction:

$\frac{1}{100}$

common fraction

0.01

decimal fraction

10. **A.** What does the denominator mean in the fraction $\frac{1}{100}$?
     B. What does the numerator mean in the fraction $\frac{1}{100}$?
     C. In the decimal 0.01 what do the zeros mean?

After Jackie finished putting her pennies into piles of 100, she found that she had 28 pennies (28¢) left over. These 28 pennies are a fraction of a dollar. We can write it as a common fraction ($\frac{28}{100}$) or a decimal fraction (0.28). We say: twenty-eight hundredths.

11. **A.** Jackie found 14 pennies in the bottom of her desk drawer. What fraction of a dollar does this represent?
     B. Write this fraction as a decimal.

12. **A.** Frank knows there are 100 centimeters in a meter. That means that the length of one centimeter is $\frac{1}{100}$ or 0.01 of a meter. Frank's pencil is 15 cm long. What fraction of a meter is the length of the pencil?

```
|||||||||||||||||||||||||||||||||||||||||||||||||||||||||||||||||||||||||||||||
   10    20    30    40    50    60    70    80    90   1M
|||||||||||||||||||||||||||||||||||||||||||||||||||||||||||||||||||||||||||||||
```
↑
15 cm   100 centimeters = 1 meter

     B. Write this number as a decimal.

Irma wants to use base-ten pieces to show hundredths. The flat is 1 whole.

13. Which base-ten piece should Irma use to show one-hundredth? Explain why you chose the piece you did.

14. **A.** How many hundredths does a skinny represent? Write this number as a common fraction and as a decimal fraction.

    B. How many hundredths does a flat represent? Write this number three ways.

Nicholas used the following base-ten pieces to show a number.

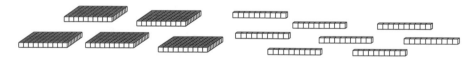

If a flat is one whole, these pieces show 3 wholes, 5 tenths, and 7 hundredths. We can write $3\frac{57}{100}$ or 3.57 for this number. We read both $3\frac{57}{100}$ and 3.57 as "Three and fifty-seven hundredths."

15. **A.** Irma places the following base-ten pieces on her desk. If a flat is one whole, then what mixed number do these pieces represent?

    B. Write this number as a decimal.

16. One student recorded 5.80 and one student recorded 5.8 for these pieces. Explain why both students are correct.

17. Get a handful of mixed skinnies and bits and count them by hundredths. Count the skinnies first (ten-hundredths, twenty-hundredths, thirty-hundredths, . . .) and then count on for the bits. When you finish, write the number for your handful.

Blackline Master

Making a Hundredths Chart

Professor Peabody made a hundredths chart. He forgot to fill in some of the chart.

Help Professor Peabody by filling in the missing values.

0.01	0.02				0.06				0.1
	0.12			0.15			0.18		
0.21			0.24			0.27			
0.31		0.33			0.36				0.4
				0.45			0.48		
	0.52								
0.61				0.65				0.69	0.7
		0.73			0.76			0.79	
0.81							0.88		0.9
0.91		0.93				0.97			1

18. What number comes after 0.09? Why is it recorded as 0.1?

19. What number comes after 0.99?

20. Describe any patterns that you see in the hundredths chart.

Centiwheel Disks

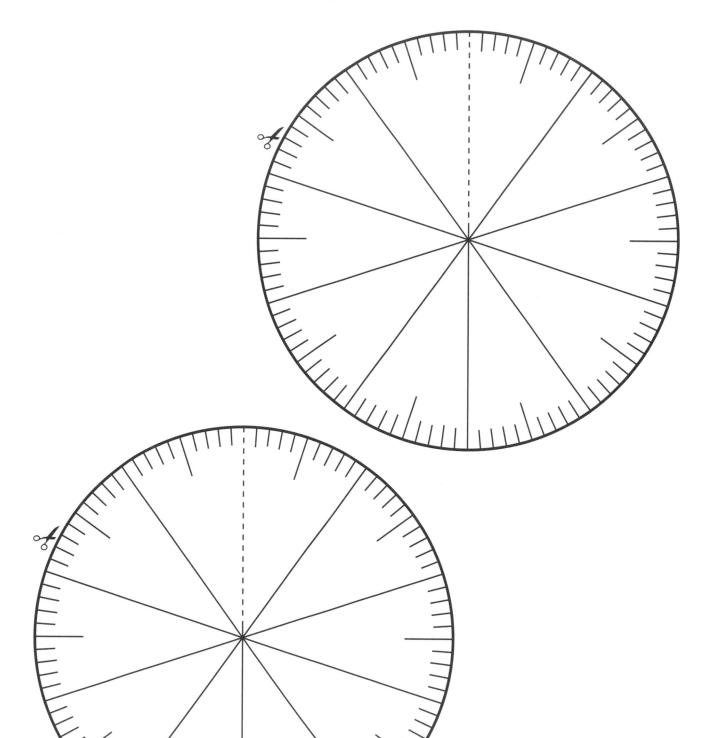

Small Centiwheels

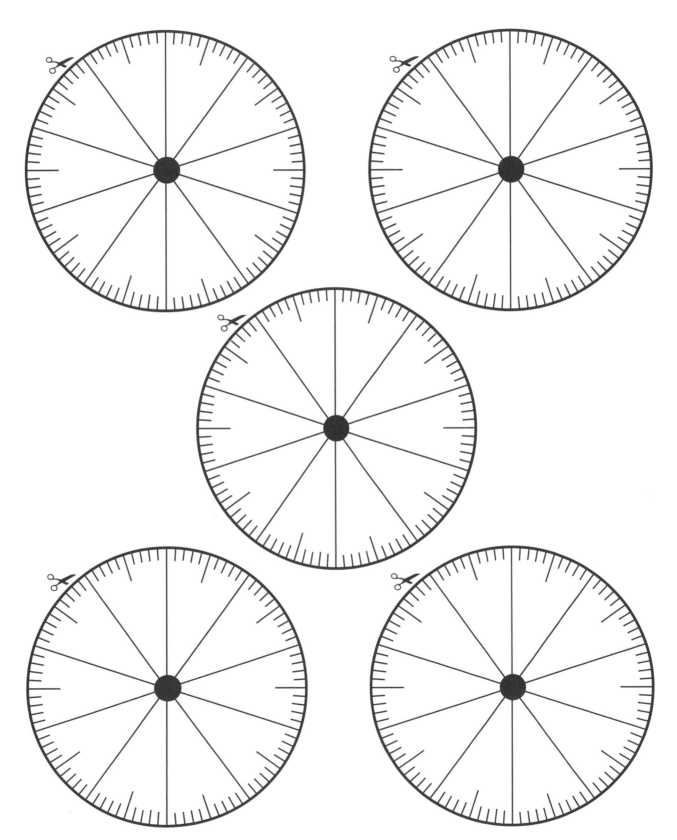

Name _____   Date _____

_____

	Trial 1	Trial 2	Trial 3	Average

Three-trial Data Table, Blackline Master

Student Guide (pp. 222–223)

1. **A.** 10

   B. $\frac{1}{10}$

2. **A.** 100

   B. $\frac{1}{100}$

3. $\frac{1}{4} = \frac{1 \times 25}{4 \times 25} = \frac{25}{100}$*

4. **A.***

   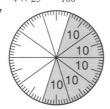

   B. $\frac{50}{100}$

5. **A.***

   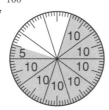

   B. $\frac{75}{100}$

6. 0.5 or 0.50, 50%*

7. 0.75, 75%*

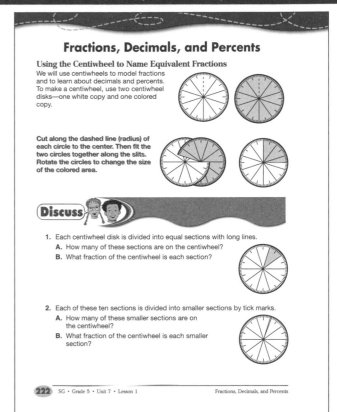

Student Guide - page 222

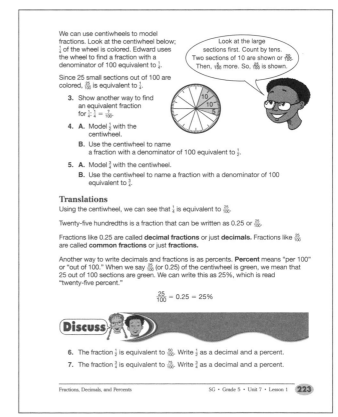

Student Guide - page 223

*Answers and/or discussion are included in the Lesson Guide.

8. **A.** Model the fraction $\frac{1}{10}$ using the centiwheel.
   B. Using the centiwheel, name a fraction with a denominator of 100 equivalent to $\frac{1}{10}$.
   C. Write $\frac{1}{10}$ as a decimal.
   D. Write $\frac{1}{10}$ as a percent.

9. **A.** Model $\frac{1}{20}$ using the centiwheel. $\frac{1}{20} = \frac{?}{100}$
   B. Write $\frac{1}{20}$ as a decimal.
   C. Write $\frac{1}{20}$ as a percent.

10. **A.** Model $\frac{1}{5}$ using the centiwheel. $\frac{1}{5} = \frac{?}{100}$
    B. Write $\frac{1}{5}$ as a decimal.
    C. Write $\frac{1}{5}$ as a percent.

11. Model each fraction with a centiwheel. Then write each fraction as a percent.
    A. $\frac{36}{100}$ **B.** $\frac{1}{2}$ **C.** $\frac{6}{100}$ **D.** $\frac{2}{5}$

12. Model each percent using a centiwheel. Then write each percent as a fraction with a denominator of 100.
    A. 95%   **B.** 70%   **C.** 7%

13. Model each decimal on the centiwheel. Write each decimal as a fraction with a denominator of 100.
    A. 0.80   **B.** 0.08   **C.** 0.85

14. Write each decimal as a percent.
    A. 0.80   **B.** 0.08   **C.** 0.85

Using the Centiwheel to Compare Fractions
15. **A.** Model 43% using the centiwheel.
    B. Is 43% closer to $\frac{1}{4}$, $\frac{1}{2}$, or 1 whole?

16. **A.** Model 0.79 using the centiwheel.
    B. Is 0.79 closer to $\frac{1}{2}$, $\frac{3}{4}$, or 1 whole?

17. **A.** Model $\frac{21}{100}$ using the centiwheel.
    B. Is $\frac{21}{100}$ closer to 0, $\frac{1}{4}$, or $\frac{1}{2}$?

Student Guide - page 224

Using the Small Centiwheel
Look at the circle graph at the right. We can use a small centiwheel to translate the fractions $\frac{1}{20}$, $\frac{7}{20}$, and $\frac{3}{5}$ to fractions with a denominator of 100.

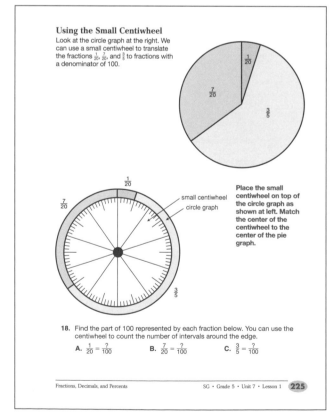

small centiwheel
circle graph

Place the small centiwheel on top of the circle graph as shown at left. Match the center of the centiwheel to the center of the pie graph.

18. Find the part of 100 represented by each fraction below. You can use the centiwheel to count the number of intervals around the edge.
    A. $\frac{1}{20} = \frac{?}{100}$ **B.** $\frac{7}{20} = \frac{?}{100}$ **C.** $\frac{3}{5} = \frac{?}{100}$

Student Guide - page 225

Student Guide (pp. 224–225)

8. **A.** See Figure 9 in Lesson Guide 1.*
   B. $\frac{1}{10} = \frac{10}{100}$*
   C. 0.1 or 0.10
   D. 10%

9. **A.** See Figure 10 in Lesson Guide 1. $\frac{1}{20} = \frac{5}{100}$*
   B. 0.05
   C. 5%

10. **A.** See Figure 11 in Lesson Guide 1. $\frac{1}{5} = \frac{20}{100}$*
    B. 0.2 or 0.20
    C. 20%

11. **A.** 36%
    B. 50%
    C. 6%
    D. 40%

12. **A.** $\frac{95}{100}$
    B. $\frac{70}{100}$
    C. $\frac{7}{100}$

13. **A.** $\frac{80}{100}$
    B. $\frac{8}{100}$
    C. $\frac{85}{100}$

14. **A.** 80%
    B. 8%
    C. 85%

15. **B.** Closer to $\frac{1}{2}$

16. **B.** Closer to $\frac{3}{4}$

17. **B.** Closer to $\frac{1}{4}$

18. **A.** $\frac{1}{20} = \frac{5}{100}$*
    B. $\frac{7}{20} = \frac{35}{100}$
    C. $\frac{3}{5} = \frac{60}{100}$

*Answers and/or discussion are included in the Lesson Guide.

Student Guide (p. 226)

19. $\frac{1}{2} = \frac{50}{100}$, $\frac{1}{4} = \frac{25}{100}$, $\frac{1}{8}$ is about $\frac{13}{100}$

$\frac{1}{10} = \frac{10}{100}$, $\frac{2}{10} = \frac{20}{100}$, $\frac{3}{10} = \frac{30}{100}$, $\frac{4}{10} = \frac{40}{100}$

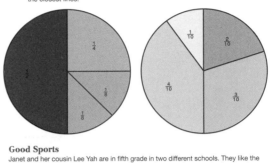

19. Use the small centiwheel. Find fractions with denominators of 100 that are close or equivalent to the fractions in the two circle graphs below. If the lines on the centiwheel do not match lines on the circle graphs exactly, use the closest lines.

Good Sports

Janet and her cousin Lee Yah are in fifth grade in two different schools. They like the same kind of books and clothes. However, they disagree about one topic—sports.

They argued about soccer and volleyball. Aunt Carol suggested that they each take a survey of their classmates' favorite sports. Later, Aunt Carol found an article which said that baseball, basketball, football, soccer, and volleyball are the 5 most popular sports in high school. The girls agreed to use these sports for their survey.

"I love volleyball, and all the kids in my class like volleyball more than soccer."

"I love soccer, and all the kids that I know agree that soccer is the best sport."

226 SG • Grade 5 • Unit 7 • Lesson 1   Fractions, Decimals, and Percents

Student Guide - page 226

Student Guide (p. 228)

20. Answers may vary slightly.

Team Sport	Lee Yah's Data			
	Fraction on Circle Graph	Nearest $\frac{N}{100}$	Decimal	Percent
Baseball	$\frac{3}{22}$	$\frac{14}{100}$	0.14	14%
Basketball	$\frac{7}{22}$	$\frac{32}{100}$	0.32	32%
Football	$\frac{2}{22}$	$\frac{9}{100}$	0.09	9%
Soccer	$\frac{4}{22}$	$\frac{18}{100}$	0.18	18%
Volleyball	$\frac{6}{22}$	$\frac{27}{100}$	0.27	27%

21. Answers may vary slightly.

Team Sport	Janet's Data			
	Fraction on Circle Graph	Nearest $\frac{N}{100}$	Decimal	Percent
Baseball	$\frac{12}{37}$	$\frac{33}{100}$	0.33	33%
Basketball	$\frac{5}{37}$	$\frac{13}{100}$	0.13	13%
Football	$\frac{6}{37}$	$\frac{16}{100}$	0.16	16%
Soccer	$\frac{7}{37}$	$\frac{19}{100}$	0.19	19%
Volleyball	$\frac{7}{37}$	$\frac{19}{100}$	0.19	19%

22.–23. Answers will vary.

Homework

1. **A.** 4%

   B. 26%

   C. 40%

20. Use a *Three-trial Data Table*. Set up the table like the one below.
   • First record in your table each sport and the fraction of students that selected that sport in Lee Yah's survey.
   • Then, use your small centiwheel to find fractions with denominators of 100 that are close to the fractions in the circle graph. Record these fractions in the column labeled "nearest $\frac{N}{100}$."
   • Record these new fractions as decimals and percents. The first one is done for you as an example.

Team Sport	Lee Yah's Data			
	Fraction on Circle Graph	Nearest $\frac{N}{100}$	Decimal (to the nearest hundredth)	Percent (to the nearest percent)
Baseball	$\frac{3}{22}$	$\frac{14}{100}$	0.14	14%
Basketball				
Football				
Soccer				
Volleyball				

21. Complete a second table for Janet's data.

22. Check your work by adding up the numbers in the percent column in both your tables. Are your totals equal to 100% or close to 100%?

23. Write a summary report comparing the data collected from the two classes. Use percents to compare the results of the two surveys.

Homework

You may wish to use the centiwheel for some of these translations.

1. Write each decimal as a percent.
   A. 0.04   B. 0.26   C. 0.40

228 SG • Grade 5 • Unit 7 • Lesson 1   Fractions, Decimals, and Percents

Student Guide - page 228

2. Write each percent as a fraction with a denominator of 100.
   A. 59%   **B.** 8%   **C.** 30%

3. Write each decimal as a fraction with a denominator of 100.
   A. 0.50   **B.** 0.07   **C.** 0.68

4. Write each fraction as a percent.
   A. $\frac{27}{100}$ **B.** $\frac{4}{100}$ **C.** $\frac{1}{2}$ **D.** $\frac{3}{20}$

5. Write each fraction as a fraction with a denominator of 100.
   A. $\frac{1}{4}$ **B.** $\frac{1}{2}$ **C.** $\frac{3}{5}$ **D.** $\frac{3}{10}$ **E.** $\frac{9}{20}$

Quilt Designs

Mr. Moreno's classroom is making a quilt for a class project. They plan to make the quilt with 100 squares of material. They have 50 blue squares, 30 red squares, 25 yellow squares, 25 orange squares, and 9 green squares to choose from. After each student designs a quilt, the class will vote to choose one pattern for the class. Here are Lin's and John's designs.

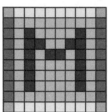 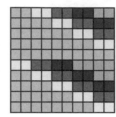

Use the *Designing Quilts* Activity Page in the *Discovery Assignment Book* to design a quilt. You will use your quilt design in the next lesson.

- You must use all five colors: blue, red, yellow, orange, and green.
- You may use no more than 50 blue, 30 red, 25 yellow, 25 orange, and 9 green squares.

Fractions, Decimals, and Percents   SG • Grade 5 • Unit 7 • Lesson 1   **229**

Student Guide - page 229

Student Guide (p. 229)

2. A. $\frac{59}{100}$

   B. $\frac{8}{100}$

   C. $\frac{30}{100}$

3. A. $\frac{50}{100}$

   B. $\frac{7}{100}$

   C. $\frac{68}{100}$

4. A. 27%

   B. 4%

   C. 50%

   D. 15%

5. A. $\frac{25}{100}$

   B. $\frac{5}{100}$

   C. $\frac{60}{100}$

   D. $\frac{30}{100}$

   E. $\frac{45}{100}$

Name _____   Date _____

Unit 7   Home Practice

PART 1   Triangle Flash Cards: All the Facts

Look at your *Multiplication* and *Division Facts I Know* charts. Take home your *Triangle Flash Cards* for all the facts you have not circled. With the help of a family member, use the cards to study a small group of facts (8 to 10 facts) each night.

Ask a family member to choose one flash card at a time. To quiz you on a multiplication fact, he or she should cover the corner containing the highest number. Multiply the two uncovered numbers.

To quiz you on a division fact, your family member can cover one of the smaller numbers. (One of the smaller numbers is circled. The other has a square around it.) Use the two uncovered numbers to solve a division fact.

Ask your family member to mix up the multiplication and division facts. He or she should sometimes cover the highest number, sometimes cover the circled number, and sometimes cover the number in the square.

PART 2   Practicing the Operations

Solve the following problems using paper and pencil. Estimate to be sure your answers are reasonable.

   A. 248 + 275 =   **B.** 8208 − 775 =   **C.** 26 × 54 =

   D. 893 × 5 =   **E.** 9 ⟌ 11,346   **F.** 3 ⟌ 1748

DECIMALS AND PROBABILITY   DAB • Grade 5 • Unit 7   **97**

Discovery Assignment Book - page 97

Discovery Assignment Book (p. 97)

Home Practice*

Part 2. Practicing the Operations

   A. 523

   B. 7433

   C. 1404

   D. 4465

   E. 1260 R6

   F. 582 R2

*Answers for all the Home Practice in the *Discovery Assignment Book* are at the end of the unit.

Discovery Assignment Book (p. 98)

Part 3. Fractions, Decimals, and Percents

	Fraction	Decimal	Percent
A.	$\frac{1}{4}$	.25	25%
B.	$\frac{98}{100}$	.98	98%
C.	$\frac{5}{100}$	.05	5%
D.	$\frac{16}{100}$	.16	16%
E.	$\frac{1}{2}$, $\frac{5}{10}$, or $\frac{50}{100}$	.50	50%

	Fraction	Decimal	Percent
F.	$\frac{20}{100}$	.20	20%
G.	$\frac{100}{100} = 1$	1.00	100%
H.	$\frac{1}{100}$	.01	1%
I.	$\frac{3}{4}$ or $\frac{75}{100}$	.75	75%
J.	$\frac{7}{100}$	.07	7%

Discovery Assignment Book (p. 101)

Designing Quilts

1.–2. Answers will vary.

Name _____ Date _____

PART 3 Fractions, Decimals, and Percents

Fill in the chart, writing each number as a fraction, a decimal, and a percent. The first one is done for you. Use your centiwheel if you need to.

	Fraction	Decimal	Percent		Fraction	Decimal	Percent
A.	$\frac{1}{4}$	.25	25%	F.	$\frac{20}{100}$		
B.		.98		G.		1.00	
C.	$\frac{5}{100}$			H.	$\frac{1}{100}$		
D.			16%	I.			75%
E.		.50		J.			7%

PART 4 Adding Fractions

Solve the following problems.

A. $\frac{1}{2} + \frac{1}{4} =$ B. $\frac{1}{2} + \frac{3}{4} =$

C. $\frac{1}{2} + \frac{1}{3} =$ D. $\frac{1}{2} + \frac{2}{3} =$

E. $\frac{1}{3} + \frac{1}{4} =$ F. $\frac{2}{3} + \frac{3}{4} =$

PART 5 Reading, Writing, and Ordering Decimals

Write the following numbers as decimals and then put them in order from smallest to largest.

A. thirty-seven thousandths _____

B. two hundred forty-two and four-hundredths _____

C. one hundred nine and fourteen-thousandths _____

D. six hundred sixteen-thousandths _____

DECIMALS AND PROBABILITY

Discovery Assignment Book - page 98

Name _____ Date _____

Designing Quilts

Homework

1. Design a quilt using this grid.
   - You must use all of these colors: blue, red, yellow, orange, and green.
   - You may use no more than 50 blue, 30 red, 25 yellow, 25 orange, and 9 green squares.

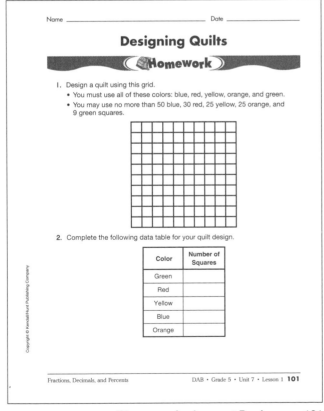

2. Complete the following data table for your quilt design.

Color	Number of Squares
Green	
Red	
Yellow	
Blue	
Orange	

Fractions, Decimals, and Percents   DAB • Grade 5 • Unit 7 • Lesson 1 **101**

Discovery Assignment Book - page 101

Tenths and Hundredths

A New Rule for Base-Ten Pieces

Doing mathematics is sometimes like playing a game. Just as you cannot play a game without rules, you cannot do mathematics without rules. But, just as people sometimes change game rules, we sometimes change rules in mathematics. And, just as we can still play a game if everyone agrees to the new rules, we can still do mathematics if everyone agrees to the new rules.

Now we are going to change a rule for base-ten pieces. When you worked with base-ten pieces before, usually a bit was one whole. When a bit is the unit, then a skinny is 10 units and a flat is 100 units. Now we are going to change which piece is the whole. **For now, a flat will be one whole.**

1. Use skinnies to cover a flat.
   A. How many skinnies did you use?
   B. If a flat is 1 whole, then what fraction is a skinny?

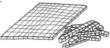

One-tenth is a fraction that can be written as 0.1 or $\frac{1}{10}$. Fractions like $\frac{1}{10}$ are called "common fractions" or just "fractions." Fractions like 0.1 are called "decimal fractions" or just "decimals." The decimal point tells us that the numbers to the right of the decimal point are smaller than 1.

$$\frac{1}{10} \begin{array}{l} \leftarrow \text{numerator} \\ \leftarrow \text{denominator} \end{array} \qquad \begin{array}{c} 0.1 \\ \uparrow \\ \text{decimal point} \end{array}$$

2. A. Place 7 skinnies on your flat. Skip count by tenths as you place each skinny. Start like this: one-tenth, two-tenths, three-tenths. . . .

   B. What fraction of the flat is 7 skinnies?

   C. Write this fraction as a common fraction and a decimal fraction.

3. A. Put 5 skinnies on your flat. Skip count by tenths as you place each skinny.

   B. Write this number as a fraction. What is another name for this fraction?

   C. Write this number as a decimal.

Unit Resource Guide - page 42

Tenths Helper Chart

You can use the Tenths Helper Chart to show how many tenths are in 1 and 2 wholes.
4. A. Cover your Tenths Helper Chart with flats. How many flats did you use?
   B. What number does this represent?

Unit Resource Guide - page 43

Unit Resource Guide (p. 42)

Tenths and Hundredths

1. A. 10
   B. $\frac{1}{10}$

2. B. seven-tenths
   C. $\frac{7}{10}$, 0.7

3. B. $\frac{5}{10}$ or $\frac{1}{2}$
   C. 0.5

Unit Resource Guide (p. 43)

4. A. 2
   B. 2

Unit Resource Guide (pp. 44–45)

5. B. Answers will vary. Possible solutions are $\frac{10}{10}$, 1.0, or 1.

6. $1 = 1.0$ since zero represents no tenths. The 10 in the denominator means the whole is divided into ten parts and the 10 in the numerator means we are interested in all ten parts.

7. A. eleven-tenths or one and one-tenth

B. 20

C. 20

8.–9.

0.1	$\frac{1}{10}$
0.2	$\frac{2}{10}$
0.3	$\frac{3}{10}$
0.4	$\frac{4}{10}$
0.5	$\frac{5}{10}$
0.6	$\frac{6}{10}$
0.7	$\frac{7}{10}$
0.8	$\frac{8}{10}$
0.9	$\frac{9}{10}$
1.0	$\frac{10}{10}$
1.1	$1\frac{1}{10}$ $\frac{11}{10}$
1.2	$1\frac{2}{10}$ $\frac{12}{10}$
1.3	$1\frac{3}{10}$ $\frac{13}{10}$
1.4	$1\frac{4}{10}$ $\frac{14}{10}$
1.5	$1\frac{5}{10}$ $\frac{15}{10}$
1.6	$1\frac{6}{10}$ $\frac{16}{10}$
1.7	$1\frac{7}{10}$ $\frac{17}{10}$
1.8	$1\frac{8}{10}$ $\frac{18}{10}$
1.9	$1\frac{9}{10}$ $\frac{19}{10}$
2.0	$1\frac{10}{10}$ $\frac{20}{10}$

10. A. There are 100 parts in the whole.

B. 1 part of the whole

C. There are no ones and no tenths.

11. A. $\frac{14}{100}$ **B.** 0.14

12. A. $\frac{15}{100}$ m   **B.** 0.15 m

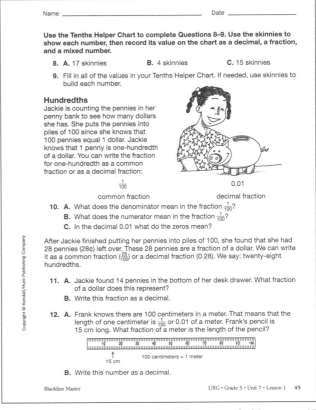

Unit Resource Guide - page 44

Unit Resource Guide - page 45

Name _____ Date _____

Irma wants to use base-ten pieces to show hundredths. The flat is 1 whole.

▭▭▭ = 1   ▭▭▭ = 0.1

13. Which base-ten piece should Irma use to show one-hundredth? Explain why you chose the piece you did.

14. A. How many hundredths does a skinny represent? Write this number as a common fraction and as a decimal fraction.

   B. How many hundredths does a flat represent? Write this number three ways.

Nicholas used the following base-ten pieces to show a number.

If a flat is one whole, these pieces show 3 wholes, 5 tenths, and 7 hundredths. We can write $3\frac{57}{100}$ or 3.57 for this number. We read both $3\frac{57}{100}$ and 3.57 as "Three and fifty-seven hundredths."

15. A. Irma places the following base-ten pieces on her desk. If a flat is one whole, then what mixed number do these pieces represent?

   B. Write this number as a decimal.

16. One student recorded 5.80 and one student recorded 5.8 for these pieces. Explain why both students are correct.

17. Get a handful of mixed skinnies and bits and count them by hundredths. Count the skinnies first (ten-hundredths, twenty-hundredths, thirty-hundredths, . . .) and then count on for the bits. When you finish, write the number for your handful.

46　URG • Grade 5 • Unit 7 • Lesson 1　　Blackline Master

Unit Resource Guide - page 46

Unit Resource Guide (p. 46)

13. One bit. There are one hundred bits in a flat. Since a flat is a whole, one bit represents one hundredth.

14. A. ten hundredths, $\frac{10}{100}$, .10

   B. hundred hundredths, $\frac{100}{100}$, 1.00, 100%

15. A. $2\frac{3}{100}$

   B. 2.03

16. In both numbers, there are 5 ones, 8 tenths, and no (0) hundredths.

17. Answers will vary.

Name _____ Date _____

Making a Hundredths Chart

Professor Peabody made a hundredths chart. He forgot to fill in some of the chart.

Help Professor Peabody by filling in the missing values.

0.01	0.02			0.06			0.1
	0.12		0.15		0.18		
0.21		0.24		0.27			
0.31	0.33		0.36			0.4	
		0.45		0.48			
	0.52						
0.61		0.65			0.69	0.7	
	0.73		0.76		0.79		
0.81				0.88		0.9	
0.91	0.93		0.97			1	

18. What number comes after 0.09? Why is it recorded as 0.1?

19. What number comes after 0.99?

20. Describe any patterns that you see in the hundredths chart.

Blackline Master　　　　URG • Grade 5 • Unit 7 • Lesson 1　47

Unit Resource Guide - page 47

Unit Resource Guide (p. 47)

18. 0.1, 0.1 is the same as 0.10.

19. 1

20. Answers will vary.

Lesson 2

Decimal Models

Lesson Overview

Students use area models to review tenths and hundredths and to explore thousandths. They use a place value chart to help them read and write decimals.

Key Content

- Translating between different representations of decimals (pictorial, symbolic).
- Understanding place value.
- Reading and writing decimals to the thousandths.
- Developing number sense for decimals.
- Comparing and ordering decimals.

Key Vocabulary

- hundredths
- ten-thousandths
- tenths
- thousandths

Homework

1. Assign the questions in the Homework section in the *Student Guide.* Students will need a *Decimal Grids* Activity Page to complete the homework.
2. Assign the game *Score One.*
3. Assign Part 4 of the Home Practice.

Assessment

Use some of the homework questions as an assessment.

Curriculum Sequence

Before This Unit

Students explored decimals in Unit 15 of third grade and Unit 10 of fourth grade. In both grades they modeled decimals with base-ten pieces. In third grade they used decimals to measure to the nearest tenth of a centimeter and in fourth grade they used decimals to measure to the nearest hundredth of a meter.

After This Unit

In Unit 8 students will use decimals and percents to compare data in the assessment lab *Comparing Lives of Animals and Soap Bubbles.* In Unit 9 they will use division to change fractions to decimals.

Materials List

Supplies and Copies

Student	Teacher
Supplies for Each Student • scissors, optional • toothpick, optional	**Supplies**
Copies • 2 copies of *Decimal Grids* per student (*Unit Resource Guide* Page 70)	**Copies/Transparencies** • 1 transparency of *Decimal Place Value Chart,* optional (*Unit Resource Guide* Page 69) • 1 transparency of *Decimal Grids,* optional (*Unit Resource Guide* Page 70)

All blackline masters including assessment, transparency, and DPP masters are also on the Teacher Resource CD.

Student Books

Decimal Models (*Student Guide* Pages 230–237)
Score One (*Discovery Assignment Book* Page 103), optional

Daily Practice and Problems and Home Practice

DPP items E–F (*Unit Resource Guide* Page 19)
Home Practice Part 4 (*Discovery Assignment Book* Page 98)

Note: Classrooms whose pacing differs significantly from the suggested pacing of the units should use the Math Facts Calendar in Section 4 of the *Facts Resource Guide* to ensure students receive the complete math facts program.

Daily Practice and Problems

Suggestions for using the DPPs are on page 67.

E. Bit: Greater Than, Less Than, or Equal To (URG p. 19)

Replace the *n* to make each sentence true.

A. $\frac{2}{3} = \frac{n}{6}$

B. $\frac{1}{3} < \frac{n}{3}$

C. $50\% = \frac{n}{10}$

D. $50\% < \frac{n}{4}$

E. $2\frac{2}{3} > 2\frac{2}{n}$

F. $20\% < \frac{n}{100}$

F. Task: *Digits Game* (URG p. 19)

Draw boxes like these on your paper.

$$\square\,\square\,.\,\square\,\square\,\square$$

As your teacher or classmate chooses digits from a deck of digit cards, place them in the boxes. Try to make the largest number. Remember that each digit will be read only once. Once you place a digit, it cannot be moved.

Decimal Models

David's Homework
Here are David's quilt design and his homework data table.

Color	Number of Squares
Green	2
Red	26
Yellow	24
Blue	28
Orange	20

He used the information from his homework table to fill in the table at the right.

Fractions, Decimals, and Percents

Color	Common Fraction	Decimal	Percent
Green	$\frac{2}{100}$	0.02	2%
Red	$\frac{26}{100}$	0.26	26%
Yellow	$\frac{24}{100}$	0.24	24%
Blue	$\frac{28}{100}$	0.28	28%
Orange	$\frac{20}{100}$	0.20	20%

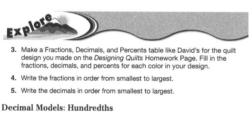 **Discuss**

1. Say each decimal in David's table out loud. For example, for 0.26 say, "twenty-six hundredths."

2. List the decimals in David's table in order from smallest to largest.

Decimal Models

Student Guide - page 230 (Answers on p. 71)

Explore

3. Make a Fractions, Decimals, and Percents table like David's for the quilt design you made on the *Designing Quilts* Homework Page. Fill in the fractions, decimals, and percents for each color in your design.

4. Write the fractions in order from smallest to largest.

5. Write the decimals in order from smallest to largest.

Decimal Models: Hundredths
In this unit you will use grids to model decimals. The large square on the left will represent one whole.

 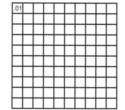

6. **A.** How many small squares are there on a 10 × 10 grid?
   B. What fraction does each small square represent?

Student Guide - page 231 (Answers on p. 71)

Before the Activity

Students will need their completed homework from Lesson 1, the *Designing Quilts* Homework Page in the *Discovery Assignment Book*. Directions and examples are in the Homework section of the *Student Guide* pages for Lesson 1 *Fractions, Decimals, and Percents*.

Teaching the Activity

Part 1   **David's Homework**

To begin the activity, students read and discuss *Questions 1–2* on the *Decimal Models* Activity Pages in the *Student Guide*. These questions refer to an example of a quilt designed on a 10 × 10 grid for homework. *Question 3* asks students to fill out a similar table using the quilt designs they completed for homework on the *Designing Quilts* Homework Page. Then students order the fractions and decimals in their tables from smallest to largest *(Questions 4–5)*.

Part 2   **Decimal Grids**

Questions 6–14 introduce students to modeling decimals with grids. For many activities in this unit, a square represents one whole as shown in Figure 13. When the square is divided into 100 smaller squares as in the *Quilt Designs* homework activity, each small square represents one-hundredth.

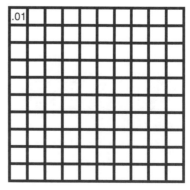

Figure 13: *Modeling hundredths*

Questions 9–10 use grids to model tenths as shown in Figure 14. Each long, thin rectangle represents one-tenth. Ask students:

- *How many small squares fit into one long, thin rectangle? That is, how many hundredths make one-tenth?* (Since 10 small squares make one thin rectangle, $\frac{10}{100} = \frac{1}{10}$ and 0.1 = 0.10 = 10%.)

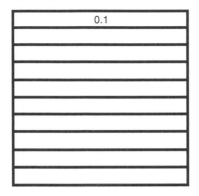

Figure 14: *A square divided into tenths*

Questions 11–14 introduce students to grids divided into thousandths as shown in Figure 15.

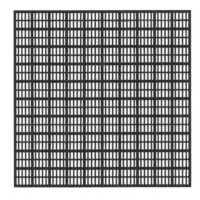

Figure 15: *A square divided into thousandths*

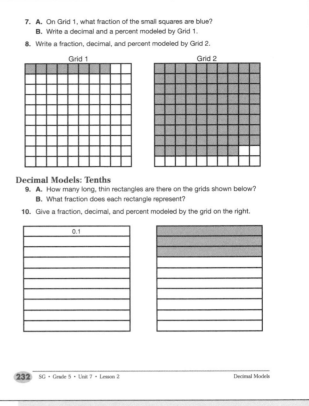

7. **A.** On Grid 1, what fraction of the small squares are blue?
   B. Write a decimal and a percent modeled by Grid 1.
8. Write a fraction, decimal, and percent modeled by Grid 2.

Grid 1   Grid 2

Decimal Models: Tenths
9. **A.** How many long, thin rectangles are there on the grids shown below?
   B. What fraction does each rectangle represent?
10. Give a fraction, decimal, and percent modeled by the grid on the right.

0.1

Student Guide - page 232 (Answers on p. 72)

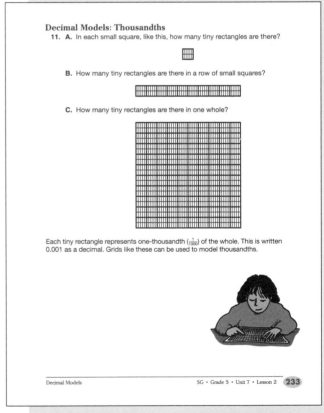

Decimal Models: Thousandths
11. **A.** In each small square, like this, how many tiny rectangles are there?

   B. How many tiny rectangles are there in a row of small squares?

   C. How many tiny rectangles are there in one whole?

Each tiny rectangle represents one-thousandth ($\frac{1}{1000}$) of the whole. This is written 0.001 as a decimal. Grids like these can be used to model thousandths.

Student Guide - page 233 (Answers on p. 72)

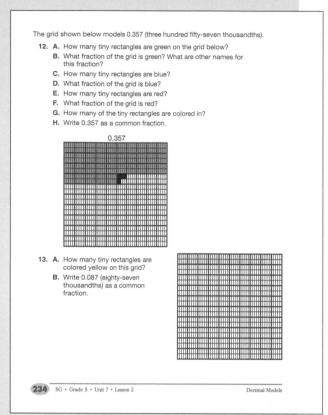

The grid shown below models 0.357 (three hundred fifty-seven thousandths).

12. A. How many tiny rectangles are green on the grid below?
    B. What fraction of the grid is green? What are other names for this fraction?
    C. How many tiny rectangles are blue?
    D. What fraction of the grid is blue?
    E. How many tiny rectangles are red?
    F. What fraction of the grid is red?
    G. How many of the tiny rectangles are colored in?
    H. Write 0.357 as a common fraction.

0.357

13. A. How many tiny rectangles are colored yellow on this grid?
    B. Write 0.087 (eighty-seven thousandths) as a common fraction.

234   SG • Grade 5 • Unit 7 • Lesson 2   Decimal Models

Student Guide - page 234 (Answers on p. 73)

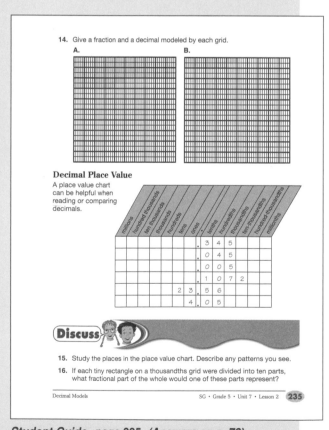

14. Give a fraction and a decimal modeled by each grid.
    A.   B.

Decimal Place Value
A place value chart can be helpful when reading or comparing decimals.

Discuss

15. Study the places in the place value chart. Describe any patterns you see.

16. If each tiny rectangle on a thousandths grid were divided into ten parts, what fractional part of the whole would one of these parts represent?

Decimal Models   SG • Grade 5 • Unit 7 • Lesson 2   235

Student Guide - page 235 (Answers on p. 73)

Question 12 refers to a grid that models 0.357. Three hundred tiny rectangles of the thousandths grid are green or 0.300 ($\frac{300}{1000}$) of the square is green. We can also say that 30 small squares are colored green or 0.30 ($\frac{30}{100}$) of the square is green and that 3 long, thin rectangles are green, so 0.3 ($\frac{3}{10}$) of the square is green. Since 50 tiny rectangles or 5 small squares are colored blue, 0.050 ($\frac{50}{1000}$) or 0.05 ($\frac{5}{100}$) of the square is blue. Finally, 7 tiny rectangles are colored red, so 0.007 of the square is red.

Question 12G asks how many tiny rectangles are colored. There are 300 green, 50 blue, and 7 red or 357 tiny rectangles that are colored. So, three hundred fifty-seven thousandths (0.357) of the square is colored in. Students can think of this as 0.3 green, 0.05 blue, and 0.007 red.

Part 3   Decimal Place Value

Use a transparency of the *Decimal Place Value Chart* or the place value chart in the Decimal Place Value section of the *Student Guide* to help students think about the 10-to-1 patterns in our place value system.

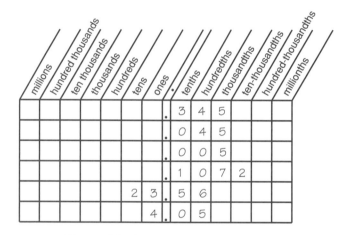

Figure 16: *Decimal place value chart*

Encourage students to look for patterns in the places in the decimal place value chart and to recognize that the place value system continues indefinitely in both directions *(Question 15)*. They should see the 10-to-1 relationship between the values of any two adjacent positions, regardless of the direction from the decimal point.

Question 16 then directs students to mentally divide each cell in the thousandths grid into ten parts to help them build a mental image of the magnitude of one ten-thousandth.

To help students read decimals, write numbers on the transparency of the *Decimal Place Value Chart* and ask students to read the numbers out loud. *Questions 17–18* ask students to read and write decimals using the decimal place value chart.

Question 19 refers to a grid as in Figure 17.

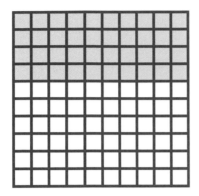

Figure 17: *10 × 10 grid*

Students can explain that 0.4, 0.40, and 40% all represent the same fraction in several ways. For example, they can use equivalent fractions:

$$\frac{4}{10} = \frac{4 \times 10}{10 \times 10} = \frac{40}{100} \qquad 0.4 = 0.40$$

Since $\frac{40}{100}$ means 40 per 100, then $\frac{40}{100} = 40\%$. Alternatively, they can use a place value chart. Since 0.40 means four-tenths and no hundredths, it is the same as just 0.4.

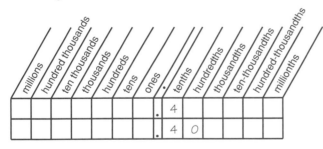

Figure 18: *Place value chart*

To complete *Question 20,* students will need one copy of the *Decimal Grids* Activity Page from the *Unit Resource Guide.*

The first four numbers written in the place value chart are less than one, since there are no digits to the left of the decimal place. To read a decimal less than one, read the number as if there were no decimal point. Then say the place value name of the last digit. For example, 0.345 is read "three hundred forty-five thousandths."

To read a decimal that is greater than one, read the whole number part. Then say "and" for the decimal point and read the decimal part. For example, 23.56 is read "twenty-three and fifty-six hundredths."

17. Read each number in the place value chart out loud.

18. Read these numbers out loud, then write them in word form.
   A. 1.5
   B. 23.567
   C. 2.06
   D. 0.432

19. Shannon wrote 0.4 for the decimal modeled by the grid below. Lee Yah wrote 0.40 for the same grid. Alexis wrote 40%. Who is correct? Explain your thinking.

236   SG • Grade 5 • Unit 7 • Lesson 2   Decimal Models

Student Guide - page 236 (Answers on p. 74)

Content Note

There are two ways to read the decimal number 0.768:

1. Read the number after the decimal point as a whole number and give it the name of its last decimal place. Read 0.768 as "seven hundred sixty-eight thousandths."

2. Read it as "point, seven-six-eight."

The first option is preferred at this time because it reinforces a knowledge of the place value system.

Decimals are often written with a leading zero that does not change the value of the number. For example, either 0.4 or .4 can represent four-tenths.

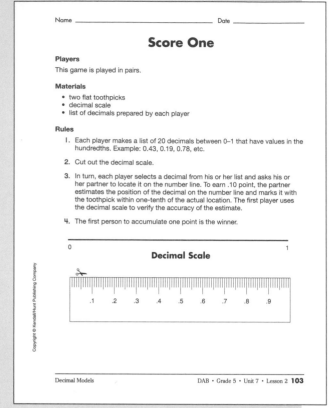

Discovery Assignment Book - page 103 *(Answers on p. 77)*

Part 4 **Introducing the Game,**
Score One **(optional)**

Introduce the game, *Score One,* in the *Discovery Assignment Book* and play it in school before assigning it as homework. This is a game for two players. To play, each student makes a list of decimals in the hundredths. Then players, taking turns and using a toothpick, estimate the placement of an opponent's decimal on a number line. Points are awarded for correct placement.

Before they begin, ask:

*   *Write three numbers between 0.5 and 0.6. Use the place value chart to help you think about what the numbers might be.*

If you need to prompt their thinking, ask:

*   *Look at the numbers 0.50 and 0.60. Now can you think of any numbers that come between these two numbers?*

If students do not come up with any numbers, refer students to a hundredths grid. Ask students:

*   *Shade 0.50 on a hundredths grid. What numbers come after 0.50 but before 0.60?*

When students are ready to list their decimals, ask them to read the directions on the *Score One* Game Page, cut out the Decimal Scale, and begin the game.

Homework and Practice

- Assign *Questions 1–5* in the Homework section. Students will need one copy of *Decimal Grids* Activity Page from the *Unit Resource Guide* to complete the homework.

- Assign the game *Score One* in the *Discovery Assignment Book* as homework.

- DPP item E can be assigned as a review of ratios, fractions, and percents. DPP item F is a game that requires number sense using decimals.

- Assign Part 4 of the Home Practice that provides practice adding fractions.

Answers for Part 4 of the Home Practice are in the Answer Key at the end of this lesson and at the end of this unit.

Assessment

Use questions in the Homework section as an assessment.

---

20. Model the numbers in the place value chart below on the *Decimal Grids* Activity Page that your teacher will give you. Label each model with the decimal it represents.

Homework

1. Show these numbers on a *Decimal Grids* Activity Page that your teacher will give you. Label each model with the decimal it represents.

   A. 0.6   B. 0.65   C. 0.653
   D. 0.8   E. 0.09   F. 0.075

2. List the decimals in order from smallest to largest.

3. Write each decimal in word form.

4. Write each decimal as a common fraction.

5. Write each of these numbers in word form.

   A. 32.76   B. 2.7
   C. 3.08   D. 3.085

Student Guide - page 237 (Answers on pp. 74–76)

Name _____ Date _____

PART 3 Fractions, Decimals, and Percents
Fill in the chart, writing each number as a fraction, a decimal, and a percent. The first one is done for you. Use your centiwheel if you need to.

	Fraction	Decimal	Percent		Fraction	Decimal	Percent
A.	$\frac{1}{4}$	.25	25%	F.	$\frac{20}{100}$		
B.		.98		G.		1.00	
C.	$\frac{5}{100}$			H.	$\frac{1}{100}$		
D.			16%	I.			75%
E.		.50		J.			7%

PART 4 Adding Fractions
Solve the following problems.

A. $\frac{1}{2} + \frac{1}{4} =$ B. $\frac{1}{2} + \frac{3}{4} =$

C. $\frac{1}{2} + \frac{1}{3} =$ D. $\frac{1}{2} + \frac{2}{3} =$

E. $\frac{1}{3} + \frac{1}{4} =$ F. $\frac{2}{3} + \frac{3}{4} =$

PART 5 Reading, Writing, and Ordering Decimals
Write the following numbers as decimals and then put them in order from smallest to largest.

A. thirty-seven thousandths _____

B. two hundred forty-two and four-hundredths _____

C. one hundred nine and fourteen-thousandths _____

D. six hundred sixteen-thousandths _____

Discovery Assignment Book - page 98 (Answers on p. 76)

At a Glance

Math Facts and Daily Practice and Problems

Use DPP items E and F to practice fractions, percents, and number sense.

Part 1. David's Homework

Use *Questions 1–5* on the *Decimal Models* Activity Pages in the *Student Guide* to begin the lesson. Students will need their homework from Lesson 1, the *Designing Quilts* Activity Page from the *Discovery Assignment Book, to complete these questions.*

Part 2. Decimal Grids

Use *Questions 6–14* in the *Student Guide* to introduce modeling decimals using grids.

Part 3. Decimal Place Value

1. Students look for patterns in the Decimal Place Value Chart in the *Student Guide. (Questions 15–16)*
2. Students use the place value chart to help them read and write decimals. *(Questions 17–18)*
3. Students explain why 0.4 = 0.40 = 40%. *(Question 19)*
4. Students model decimals on a *Decimal Grids* Activity Page from the *Unit Resource Guide. (Question 20)*

Part 4. Introducing the Game, *Score One* (optional)

Introduce the game *Score One* in the *Discovery Assignment Book* and play it in class.

Homework

1. Assign the questions in the Homework section in the *Student Guide.* Students will need a *Decimal Grids* Activity Page to complete the homework.
2. Assign the game *Score One.*
3. Assign Part 4 of the Home Practice.

Assessment

Use some of the homework questions as an assessment.

Answer Key is on pages 71–77.

Notes:

Decimal Place Value Chart

millions	hundred thousands	ten thousands	thousands	hundreds	tens	ones	.	tenths	hundredths	thousandths	ten-thousandths	hundred-thousandths	millionths
							•						
							•						
							•						
							•						
							•						
							•						

Decimal Grids

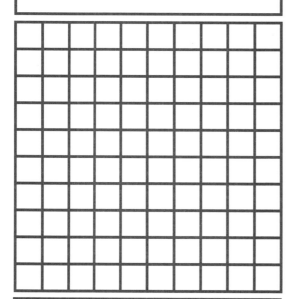
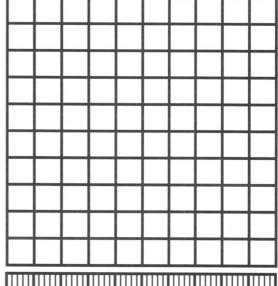
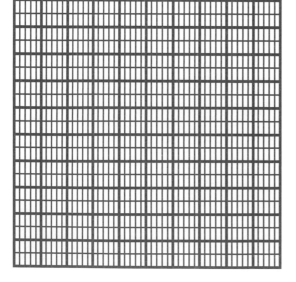
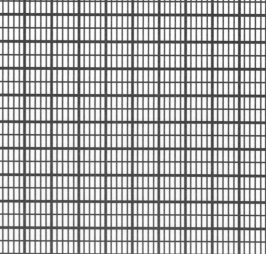

Blackline Master

Student Guide (p. 230)

Decimal Models

1. two-hundredths, twenty-four hundredths, twenty-eight hundredths, twenty-hundredths

2. 0.02, 0.20, 0.24, 0.26, 0.28

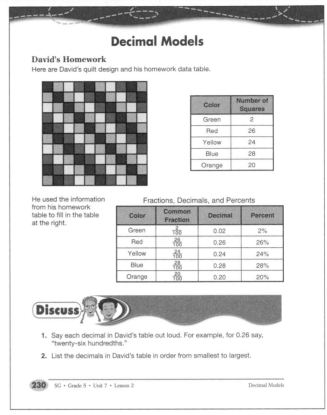

Student Guide - page 230

Student Guide (p. 231)

3.–5. Answers will vary.

6. **A.** 100

   B. $\frac{1}{100}$

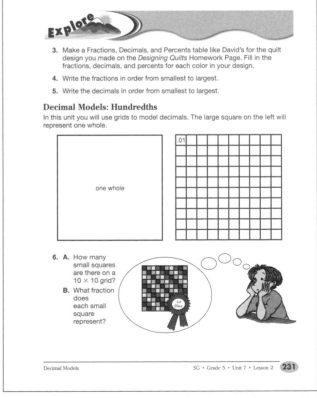

Student Guide - page 231

7. **A.** On Grid 1, what fraction of the small squares are blue?
   B. Write a decimal and a percent modeled by Grid 1.

8. Write a fraction, decimal, and percent modeled by Grid 2.

Grid 1 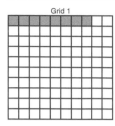   Grid 2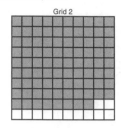

Decimal Models: Tenths

9. **A.** How many long, thin rectangles are there on the grids shown below?
   B. What fraction does each rectangle represent?

10. Give a fraction, decimal, and percent modeled by the grid on the right.

0.1

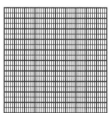

Student Guide - page 232

Student Guide (p. 232)

7. **A.** $\frac{8}{100}$

   B. 0.08, 8%

8. $\frac{88}{100}$, 0.88, 88%

9. **A.** 10*

   B. $\frac{1}{10}$

10. $\frac{3}{10}$, 0.3, 30%

Decimal Models: Thousandths

11. **A.** In each small square, like this, how many tiny rectangles are there?

   B. How many tiny rectangles are there in a row of small squares?

   C. How many tiny rectangles are there in one whole?

Each tiny rectangle represents one-thousandth ($\frac{1}{1000}$) of the whole. This is written 0.001 as a decimal. Grids like these can be used to model thousandths.

Student Guide - page 233

Student Guide (p. 233)

11. **A.** 10

    B. 100

    C. 1000

*Answers and/or discussion are included in the Lesson Guide.

Student Guide (p. 234)

12.* **A.** 300

　　B. $\frac{300}{1000}$, $\frac{30}{100}$, or $\frac{3}{10}$

　　C. 50

　　D. $\frac{50}{1000}$ or $\frac{5}{100}$

　　E. 7

　　F. $\frac{7}{1000}$

　　G. 357

　　H. $\frac{357}{1000}$

13. **A.** 87

　　B. $\frac{87}{1000}$

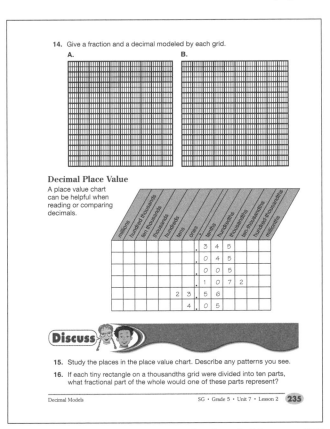

Student Guide - page 234

Student Guide (p. 235)

14. **A.** $\frac{245}{1000}$, 0.245

　　B. $\frac{45}{1000}$, 0.045

15. Answers will vary. Possible answers include: Each place has a value ten times the place to the right; except for the ones place, the names on the right side of the decimal point are the same as the names on the left, except the names on the right have a "th" on the end; and the value of the places on the left side of the chart get larger and larger as you move to the left while the places on the right side of the chart get smaller and smaller as you move to the right.*

16. one ten-thousandth $(\frac{1}{10,000})$*

Student Guide - page 235

*Answers and/or discussion are included in the Lesson Guide.

The first four numbers written in the place value chart are less than one, since there are no digits to the left of the decimal place. To read a number less than one, read the number as if there were no decimal point. Then say the place value name of the last digit. For example, 0.345 is read "three hundred forty-five thousandths."

To read a decimal that is greater than one, read the whole number part. Then say "and" for the decimal point and read the decimal part. For example, 23.56 is read "twenty-three and fifty-six hundredths."

17. Read each number in the place value chart out loud.

18. Read these numbers out loud, then write them in word form.
   A. 1.5
   B. 23.567
   C. 2.06
   D. 0.432

19. Shannon wrote 0.4 for the decimal modeled by the grid below. Lee Yah wrote 0.40 for the same grid. Alexis wrote 40%. Who is correct? Explain your thinking.

Student Guide - page 236

20. Model the numbers in the place value chart below on the *Decimal Grids* Activity Page that your teacher will give you. Label each model with the decimal it represents.

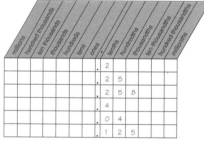

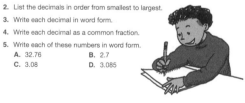

1. Show these numbers on a *Decimal Grids* Activity Page that your teacher will give you. Label each model with the decimal it represents.
   A. 0.6   B. 0.65   C. 0.653
   D. 0.8   E. 0.09   F. 0.075

2. List the decimals in order from smallest to largest.

3. Write each decimal in word form.

4. Write each decimal as a common fraction.

5. Write each of these numbers in word form.
   A. 32.76   B. 2.7
   C. 3.08   D. 3.085

Student Guide - page 237

*Answers and/or discussion are included in the Lesson Guide.

Student Guide (pp. 236–237)

17. 0.345—Three hundred forty-five thousandths

   0.045—Forty-five thousandths

   0.005—Five-thousandths

   0.1072—One thousand seventy-two ten-thousandths

   23.56—Twenty-three and fifty-six hundredths

   4.05—Four and five-hundredths

18. **A.** One and five-tenths

   B. Twenty-three and five hundred sixty-seven thousandths

   C. Two and six-hundredths

   D. Four hundred thirty-two thousandths

19. Answers will vary. See Lesson Guide 2.*

20.

0.2

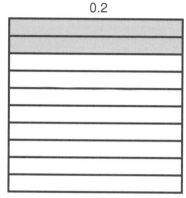

0.25

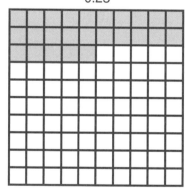

0.258

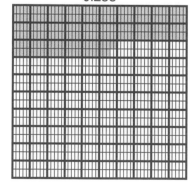

0.4

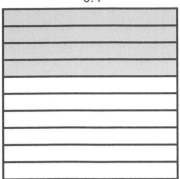

B. 0.65

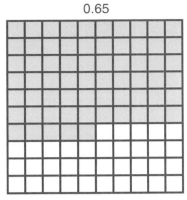

0.04

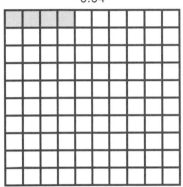

C. 0.653

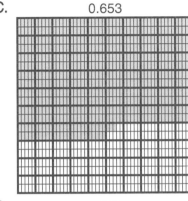

0.125

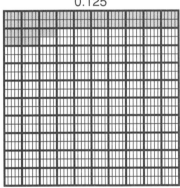

D. 0.8

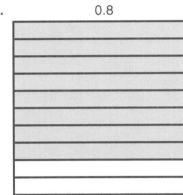

E. 0.09

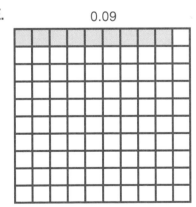

Homework

I. A. 0.6

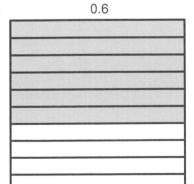

F.
0.075

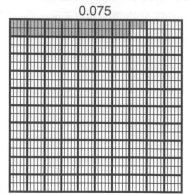

2. 0.075, 0.09, 0.6, 0.65, 0.653, 0.8

3. A. six-tenths

B. sixty-five hundredths

C. six hundred fifty-three thousandths

D. eight-tenths

E. nine-hundredths

F. seventy-five thousandths

4. A. $\frac{6}{10}$

B. $\frac{65}{100}$

C. $\frac{653}{1000}$

D. $\frac{8}{10}$

E. $\frac{9}{100}$

F. $\frac{75}{1000}$

5. A. thirty-two and seventy-six hundredths

B. two and seven-tenths

C. three and eight-hundredths

D. three and eighty-five thousandths

Name _____ Date _____

PART 3 Fractions, Decimals, and Percents

Fill in the chart, writing each number as a fraction, a decimal, and a percent.
The first one is done for you. Use your centiwheel if you need to.

	Fraction	Decimal	Percent		Fraction	Decimal	Percent
A.	$\frac{1}{4}$	.25	25%	F.	$\frac{20}{100}$		
B.		.98		G.		1.00	
C.	$\frac{5}{100}$			H.	$\frac{1}{100}$		
D.			16%	I.			75%
E.		.50		J.			7%

PART 4 Adding Fractions

Solve the following problems.

A. $\frac{1}{2} + \frac{1}{4} =$ B. $\frac{1}{2} + \frac{3}{4} =$

C. $\frac{1}{2} + \frac{1}{3} =$ D. $\frac{1}{2} + \frac{2}{3} =$

E. $\frac{1}{3} + \frac{1}{4} =$ F. $\frac{2}{3} + \frac{3}{4} =$

PART 5 Reading, Writing, and Ordering Decimals

Write the following numbers as decimals and then put them in order from
smallest to largest.

A. thirty-seven thousandths _____

B. two hundred forty-two and four-hundredths _____

C. one hundred nine and fourteen-thousandths _____

D. six hundred sixteen-thousandths _____

98 DAB • Grade 5 • Unit 7   DECIMALS AND PROBABILITY

Discovery Assignment Book - page 98

Discovery Assignment Book (p. 98)

Home Practice*

Part 4. Adding Fractions

A. $\frac{3}{4}$

B. $\frac{5}{4}$ or $1\frac{1}{4}$

C. $\frac{5}{6}$

D. $\frac{7}{6}$ or $1\frac{1}{6}$

E. $\frac{7}{12}$

F. $\frac{17}{12}$ or $1\frac{5}{12}$

*Answers for all the Home Practice in the *Discovery Assignment Book* are at the end of the unit.

Discovery Assignment Book (p. 103)

Score One

See Lesson Guide 2 for a discussion of the game.*

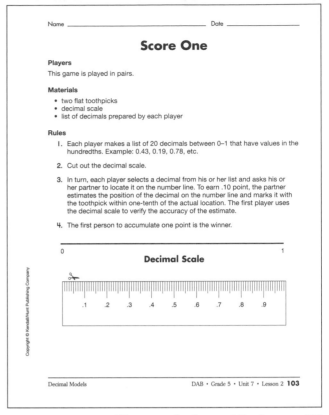

Discovery Assignment Book - page 103

---

*Answers for all the Home Practice in the *Discovery Assignment Book* are at the end of the unit.

Lesson 3

Comparing and Rounding Decimals

Estimated Class Sessions

2

Lesson Overview

In Part 1 of the lesson, students use activity pages from the *Discovery Assignment Book* to model decimals using square grids. They use these models to round and compare decimals.

Parts 2 and 3 of the lesson are in the *Student Guide*. Students use benchmarks and place value charts to compare and order decimals. They also round decimals to the nearest whole number, tenth, and hundredth. Students continue to connect fractions and decimals to percents. They will use these skills in the lab *Flipping Two Coins* in Lesson 8.

Key Content

- Comparing and ordering decimals.
- Rounding decimals.

Key Vocabulary

- benchmarks

Math Facts

DPP item G reviews the multiplication and division facts.

Homework

1. Assign the Homework section in the *Student Guide*. Students will need a copy of the *Decimal Grids* Activity Page from the *Unit Resource Guide* to complete the assignment.
2. Assign the *Connect the Dots* Activity Page in the *Discovery Assignment Book* for homework. (optional)

Assessment

Use Part 5 of the Home Practice as a quiz.

Curriculum Sequence

Before This Unit

Students used benchmarks of 0, $\frac{1}{2}$, and 1 to compare and order fractions in Lesson 4 of Unit 3.

Materials List

Supplies and Copies

Student	Teacher
Supplies for Each Student	**Supplies**
Copies	**Copies/Transparencies**
• 1–3 copies of *Decimal Grids* per student (*Unit Resource Guide* Page 70)	• 1 transparency of *Decimals: A Closer Look*, optional (*Discovery Assignment Book* Pages 105–109) • 1 transparency of *Decimal Place Value Chart* (*Unit Resource Guide* Page 69) • 1 transparency of *Decimal Grids* (*Unit Resource Guide* Page 70)

All blackline masters including assessment, transparency, and DPP masters are also on the Teacher Resource CD.

Student Books

Comparing and Rounding Decimals (*Student Guide* Pages 238–242)
Decimals: A Closer Look (*Discovery Assignment Book* Pages 105–109)
Connect the Dots (*Discovery Assignment Book* Page 111), optional

Daily Practice and Problems and Home Practice

DPP items G–J (*Unit Resource Guide Pages* 20–21)
Home Practice Part 5 (*Discovery Assignment Book* Page 98)

Note: Classrooms whose pacing differs significantly from the suggested pacing of the units should use the Math Facts Calendar in Section 4 of the *Facts Resource Guide* to ensure students receive the complete math facts program.

G. Bit: Reviewing the Facts (URG p. 20)

Solve the given fact. Then name the other related fact or facts in the same fact family.

A. $8 \times 6 =$ B. $12 \div 4 =$

C. $80 \div 8 =$ D. $40 \div 8 =$

E. $7 \times 9 =$ F. $2 \times 4 =$

H. Task: Movie Schedules (URG p. 20)

The first showing of a new comedy is at 1:20 in the afternoon. The movie is 2 hours and 15 minutes long. There is a twenty minute break between movies. There are four showings of the movie. List the starting and ending times of the four showings.

I. Bit: Skip Counting (URG p. 21)

1. Skip count by dimes to $2.00. Start like this: $0.10, $0.20, $0.30 . . .

2. Skip count by tenths to 2. Start like this: 0.1, 0.2, 0.3 . . .

3. Skip count by quarters to $5.00. Start like this: $0.25, $0.50, $0.75 . . .

4. Skip count by 0.25 (twenty-five hundredths) to 5. Start like this: 0.25, 0.50, 0.75 . . .

J. Task: Time Is Money (URG p. 21)

It is 1:50 P.M. when Nila's mother parks the car near Nila's ballet lesson. The parking meter takes 25 cents for each 15 minutes. It only takes quarters. Nila's mother has $1.75 in quarters.

1. If she uses all her quarters, what time will she need to return to her car?

2. If she wants to stay until 4:30, how much more money will she need?

Before the Activity

Play a decimal version of the *Digits Game,* described in DPP item F, as a warm-up activity.

Teaching the Activity

Part 1 Decimals: A Closer Look

> **TIMS Tip**
>
> Use the *Decimals: A Closer Look* Activity Pages in the *Discovery Assignment Book* to guide students through a teacher-led class discussion. Or, have students work in pairs or small groups to complete the pages and then report their results to the class.

Questions 1–2 ask students to model decimals on grids and then round the decimals. To help students see the nearest hundredth and thousandth, shade the decimals on a transparency. For example, for *Question 2,* students shade in 0.462 of a thousandths grid as shown in Figure 19.

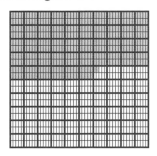

Figure 19: *Modeling 0.462 on a thousandths grid*

Shade 0.462 on a transparency of the *Decimal Grids* Activity Page from the *Unit Resource Guide* and ask:

- *Is 0.462 closer to 0.46 or 0.47?* (0.46. Finding the closest hundredth is rounding to the nearest hundredth.)
- *Round 0.462 to the nearest hundredth.* (0.46)
- *Is 0.462 closer to 4 tenths or 5 tenths?* (0.5)
- *Round 0.462 to the nearest tenth.* (0.5)

Questions 3–4 develop rounding skills that students will use in the *Flipping Two Coins* lab. In the lab, students report probabilities to the nearest percent. *Question 3* asks students to shade $\frac{572}{1000}$ on a thousandths grid. Then they round 0.572 to the nearest hundredth (0.57), and write the decimal as a percent (57%).

Questions 5–6 ask students to compare 0.3 of a grid, 0.30 of a grid, and 0.300 of a grid. Students can see that these three decimals are equal since the same area is shaded on all three grids. Ask students:

- *Is 0.30 equal to 0.3 and 0.300? How do you know?*

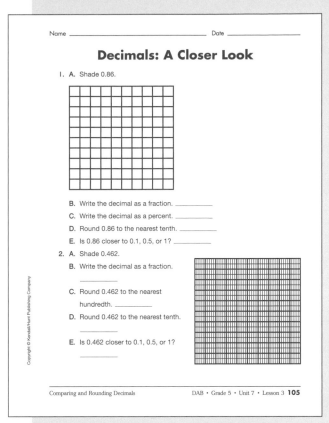

Discovery Assignment Book - page 105 *(Answers on p. 90)*

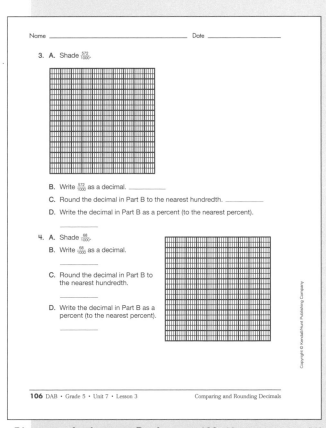

Discovery Assignment Book - page 106 *(Answers on p. 91)*

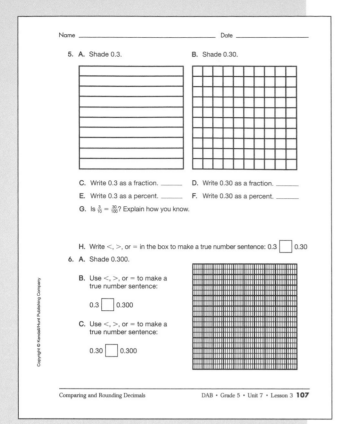

Discovery Assignment Book - page 107 *(Answers on p. 91)*

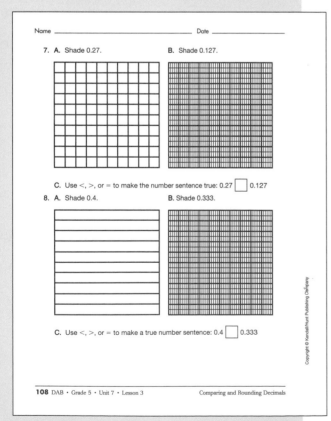

Discovery Assignment Book - page 108 *(Answers on p. 92)*

Questions 5C–5G give them another way to see that the decimals are equivalent. They write 0.3 and 0.30 as fractions. Since $\frac{3}{10} = \frac{3 \times 10}{10 \times 10} = \frac{30}{100}$, 0.3 = 0.30. With this understanding, they should see that both 0.3 and 0.30 equal 30%.

Accuracy in Measurement. When reading a measurement, 0.3 m gives us different information than 0.300 m. Writing a length measurement as 0.3 m indicates that the length was measured to the nearest tenth of a meter. We can expect errors as large as 0.05 m. Writing a measurement as 0.300 m tells us the length was measured to the nearest thousandth of a meter, a much more accurate measure.

Questions 7–8 use the area model to help students visualize decimals to compare them.

Question 9 asks students to model 1.83 using two grids. Students will need to use similar models when they use grids to add decimals in Lesson 4.

Part 2 **Comparing Decimals: Benchmarks, Place Value Charts, and Grids**

The *Comparing and Rounding Decimals* Activity Pages in the *Student Guide* begin by using benchmarks to order decimals. Students study the table shown in Figure 20.

Decimals Near or Equal to 0	Decimals Near or Equal to 0.1	Decimals Near or Equal to 0.5	Decimals Near or Equal to 1	Decimals Much Greater Than 1
0.0	0.09	0.500	0.9	3
0.0099	0.10	.48	1.0	5.26
.01	0.081	0.6	.819	30.5
0.003	0.21	0.607	1.05	7.9

Figure 20: *Sorting decimals using benchmarks of 0, 0.1, 0.5, and 1*

In *Question 1* students sort decimals in a table similar to the one shown in the *Student Guide*. *Question 2* asks students to describe how the decimals in each column are alike. Possible student responses include:

*   All the decimals near zero have zeros in the tenths place and either a zero or a 1 in the hundredths place;

*   The decimals near 0.1 have 0, 1, or 2 in the tenths place;

*   The decimals near 0.5 have a number close to five in the tenths place;

*   The decimals near or equal to 1 have a one in the ones place or an 8 or 9 in the tenths place; and

*   Decimals much greater than one have a number to the left of the decimal point that is greater than 1.

Question 3 asks students to add other decimals to the table created in **Question 1. Question 4** asks students to use these benchmarks to order decimals.

Question 5 uses a place value chart to help students compare decimals. Use a transparency of the *Decimal Place Value Chart* to guide the class discussion. Use the numbers in the *Student Guide* or write similar numbers in the table. See Figure 21.

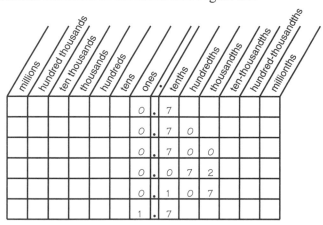

Figure 21: *Using a place value chart to compare decimals*

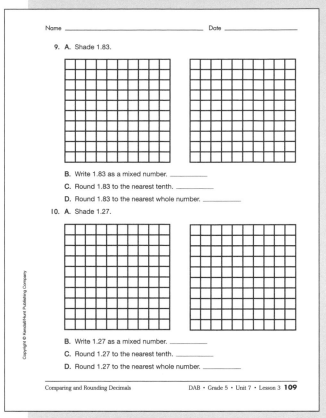

9. **A.** Shade 1.83.

B. Write 1.83 as a mixed number. _____
C. Round 1.83 to the nearest tenth. _____
D. Round 1.83 to the nearest whole number. _____

10. **A.** Shade 1.27.

B. Write 1.27 as a mixed number. _____
C. Round 1.27 to the nearest tenth. _____
D. Round 1.27 to the nearest whole number. _____

Comparing and Rounding Decimals   DAB • Grade 5 • Unit 7 • Lesson 3 **109**

Discovery Assignment Book - **page 109** *(Answers on p. 92)*

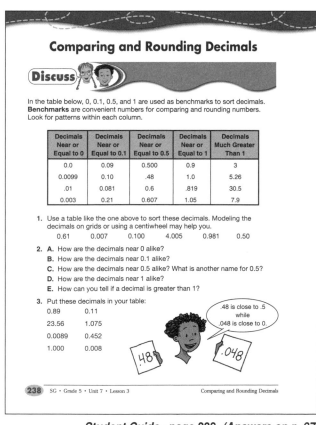

Student Guide - **page 238** *(Answers on p. 87)*

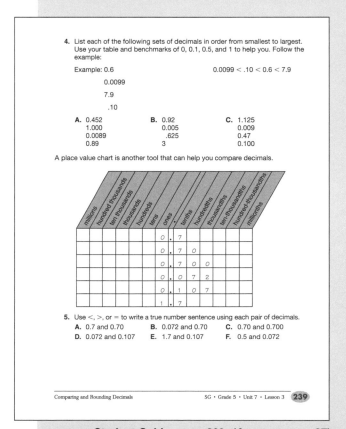

Student Guide - **page 239** *(Answers on p. 87)*

For Questions 6–7 you may use benchmarks, decimal grids, fractions, or a place value chart to help you. Explain how you found each answer.

6. Write the following sets of decimals in order from smallest to largest:
   A. 0.729   12   1.25   0.099
   B. 0.8   8.0   0.888   0.08
   C. 0.48   1.5   0.525   0.5

7. Use <, >, or = to write a true number sentence using each pair of decimals.
   A. 0.9 and 0.900
   B. 0.55 and 0.155
   C. 0.23 and 0.234

Rounding Decimals
The grid at the right shows 0.892
8. A. Is 0.892 closer to 0.89 or 0.90?
   B. Round 0.892 to the nearest hundredth.
   C. Is 0.892 closer to 0.8 or 0.9?
   D. Round 0.892 to the nearest tenth.
   E. Is 0.892 closer to 0 or 1?
   F. Round 0.892 to the nearest whole number.

9. Round each decimal to the nearest whole number.
   A. 4.32   B. 0.891   C. 19.9
   D. 1.09   E. 35.9   F. 2.58

10. Round each decimal to the nearest tenth.
   A. 4.32   B. 0.891   C. 0.199
   D. 0.109   E. 0.78   F. 1.657

11. Round each decimal to the nearest hundredth.
   A. 0.487   B. 0.531   C. 1.019
   D. 0.899   E. 3.154   F. 0.607

240   SG • Grade 5 • Unit 7 • Lesson 3   Comparing and Rounding Decimals

12. Complete the table. The first one is done for you.

	Fraction	Decimal	Decimal (to the Nearest Hundredth)	Percent (to the Nearest Percent)
A.	$\frac{254}{1000}$	0.254	.25	25%
B.	$\frac{327}{1000}$			
C.	$\frac{43}{1000}$			
D.	$\frac{789}{1000}$			
E.	$\frac{799}{1000}$			

Homework

Use a copy of the Decimal Grids Activity Page to answer Questions 1–8.

1. Shade each of the following decimals. Label each one clearly.
   A. 0.5   B. 0.87   C. 0.067
   D. 0.2   E. 0.20   F. 0.427

2. Write each of the decimals in Question 1 as a common fraction.

3. A. Write 0.5 as a percent.
   B. Write 0.2 as a percent.
   C. Write 0.20 as a percent.
   D. Write 0.87 as a percent.

4. A. Round 0.87 to the nearest tenth.
   B. Round 0.067 to the nearest tenth.
   C. Round 0.427 to the nearest tenth.

5. A. Round 0.067 to the nearest hundredth.
   B. Write 0.067 as a percent to the nearest percent.

6. A. Round 0.427 to the nearest hundredth.
   B. Write 0.427 as a percent to the nearest percent.

Comparing and Rounding Decimals   SG • Grade 5 • Unit 7 • Lesson 3   241

TIMS Tip

Point out to students that we can place a decimal after the whole number and not change the value of the number 3 = 3. = 3.0.

Ask students how they can use the chart to compare decimals. Guide students to compare the numbers one place at a time, moving from left to right. For example, ask:

- *Is 0.7 greater than, less than, or equal to 0.70? How do you know?* (0.7 = 0.70. Each number has seven tenths and no hundredths. The 0 in the hundredths place of 0.70 adds no value to the number.)

- *Is 0.7 greater than, less than, or equal to 0.072? How do you know?* (0.7 > 0.072 since there is a 7 in the tenths place in 0.7 and a 0 in the tenths place in 0.072.)

Questions 6–7 ask students to choose their own tools and strategies to order and compare decimals. Make copies of the *Decimal Grids* Activity Page available to students. Students can work in pairs to answer the questions. Then encourage students to share their strategies with the class. Ask:

- *What strategies can you use to compare decimals?*

Possible student answers are:

- Shade decimal grids.

- Picture decimal grids in your mind.

- Write the decimals as fractions. For example, to compare 0.9 and 0.90, compare $\frac{9}{10}$ to $\frac{90}{100}$. Since $\frac{9}{10} = \frac{9 \times 10}{10 \times 10} = \frac{90}{100}$, then 0.9 = 0.90.

- Use benchmarks such as 0, 0.1, 0.5, and 1.

- Rewrite each decimal with the same number of digits. For example, 2.9 > 2.82 can be written as 2.90 > 2.82.

- Think about a place value chart. Compare decimals one digit at a time from left to right. As above, 2.9 > 2.82, since 9 tenths is greater than 8 tenths and 2 hundredths.

Part 3 Rounding Decimals

Question 8 in the *Student Guide* reviews rounding decimals using the same concepts introduced in the *Decimals: A Closer Look* Activity Pages in the *Discovery Assignment Book*. Check student understanding as they work through *Questions 9–12*. Encourage students to shade the decimals on grids on the *Decimal Grids* Activity Page (or just to picture the grids) if they need help. You may want to discuss *Question 11D* using a shaded grid on a transparency: 0.899 rounded to the nearest hundredth is 0.90.

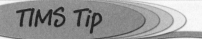

TIMS Tip

The *Decimal Grids* Activity Page is in Lesson 2.

Math Facts

DPP item G reviews the multiplication and division facts.

Homework and Practice

- Assign the Homework section in the *Student Guide*. Students will need a copy of the *Decimal Grids* Activity Page in the *Unit Resource Guide* for Lesson 2 to complete the homework.

- Assign the *Connect the Dots* Activity Page in the *Discovery Assignment Book*. (optional)

- Assign DPP items H–J to practice skip counting with decimals and solve problems about time and money.

Assessment

Use Part 5 *Reading, Writing, and Ordering Decimals* of the Home Practice as a quiz.

Answers for Part 5 of the Home Practice are in the Answer Key at the end of this lesson and at the end of this unit.

---

7. **A.** Is 0.427 closer to 0.1, 0.5, or 1?
B. Is 0.067 closer to 0.1, 0.5, or 1?
C. Is 0.87 closer to 0.1, 0.5, or 1?
D. Is 0.20 closer to 0.1, 0.5, or 1?

8. Use <, >, or = to write a true number sentence using each pair of decimals. Explain how you found each answer.
A. 0.5 and 0.427   **B.** 0.2 and 0.20   **C.** 0.87 and 0.427

9. Place the following set of decimals in order from smallest to largest:
A. 0.201   1.03   10   0.023   0.63
B. 6.01   6.10   6.4   0.6   0.06
C. 11   1.01   0.101   1.1   0.11
D. 0.487   0.88   1.08   0.098   0.5

10. Look at the decimals on the blackboard in the picture. Explain how Roberto knows that 0.327 is less than 0.37.

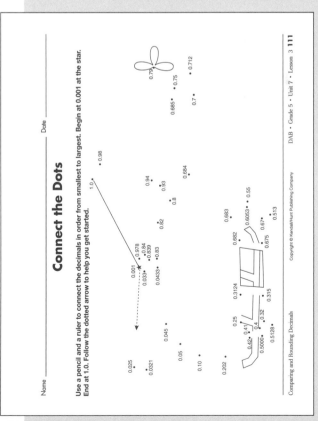

Student Guide - page 242 (Answers on p. 89)

Name _____ Date _____

PART 3 Fractions, Decimals, and Percents
Fill in the chart, writing each number as a fraction, a decimal, and a percent. The first one is done for you. Use your centiwheel if you need to.

	Fraction	Decimal	Percent		Fraction	Decimal	Percent
A.	$\frac{1}{4}$	.25	25%	F.	$\frac{20}{100}$		
B.		.98		G.		1.00	
C.	$\frac{5}{100}$			H.	$\frac{1}{100}$		
D.			16%	I.			75%
E.		.50		J.			7%

PART 4 Adding Fractions
Solve the following problems.

A. $\frac{1}{2} + \frac{1}{4} =$ B. $\frac{1}{2} + \frac{3}{4} =$

C. $\frac{1}{2} + \frac{1}{3} =$ D. $\frac{1}{2} + \frac{2}{3} =$

E. $\frac{1}{3} + \frac{1}{4} =$ F. $\frac{2}{3} + \frac{3}{4} =$

PART 5 Reading, Writing, and Ordering Decimals
Write the following numbers as decimals and then put them in order from smallest to largest.

A. thirty-seven thousandths _____
B. two hundred forty-two and four-hundredths _____
C. one hundred nine and fourteen-thousandths _____
D. six hundred sixteen-thousandths _____

Discovery Assignment Book - page 98 (Answers on p. 90)

Discovery Assignment Book - page 111 (Answers on p. 93)

At a Glance

Math Facts and Daily Practice and Problems

DPP item G reviews the facts. Items H–J involve elapsed time and skip counting with decimals.

Before the Activity

Play a decimal version of *Digits Game* as a warm-up. See DPP item F.

Part 1. *Decimals: A Closer Look*

Students complete the *Decimals: A Closer Look* Activity Pages in the *Discovery Assignment Book.*

Part 2. Comparing Decimals: Benchmarks, Place Value Charts, and Grids

1. Students use benchmarks to order decimals. They discuss *Questions 1–4* on the *Comparing and Rounding Decimals* Activity Pages in the *Student Guide.*
2. Students use place value charts to compare decimals. *(Question 5)*
3. Students choose tools to help them order and compare decimals. They discuss their strategies with the class. *(Questions 6–7)*

Part 3. Rounding Decimals

Students round decimals in *Questions 8–12* in the *Student Guide.*

Homework

1. Assign the Homework section in the *Student Guide.* Students will need a copy of the *Decimal Grids* Activity Page from the *Unit Resource Guide* to complete the assignment.
2. Assign the *Connect the Dots* Activity Page in the *Discovery Assignment Book* for homework. (optional)

Assessment

Use Part 5 of the Home Practice as a quiz.

Answer Key is on pages 87–93.

Notes:

Student Guide (pp. 238–239)

Comparing and Rounding Decimals

1. and **3.**

Decimals Near or Equal to 0	Decimals Near or Equal to 0.1	Decimals Near or Equal to 0.5	Decimals Near or Equal to 1	Decimals Much Greater Than 1
0.007	0.100	0.61	0.981	4.005
0.0089	.11	.50	0.89	23.56
.008		0.452	1.075	
			1.000	

2.* A. Answers may vary. One possible response is: All the decimals near zero have zeros in the tenths place and either a zero or a 1 in the hundredths place.

B. Answers may vary. One possible response is: All the decimals near 0.1 have 0, 1, or 2 in the tenths place.

C. Answers may vary. One possible response is: All the decimals near 0.5 have numbers close to five in the tenths place. Another name for 0.5 is $\frac{1}{2}$.

D. Answers may vary. One possible response is: All the decimals near 1 have a 1 in the ones place and 0, 1, or 2 in the tenths place. Or, if they do not have a 1 in the ones place, they have an 8 or 9 in the tenths place.

E. Answers may vary. One possible response is: A decimal is much greater than 1 if there is a digit greater than one to the left of the decimal. Or if the number in the ones place is greater than 1.

3. See table for *Question 1.*

4. A. $0.0089 < 0.452 < 0.89 < 1.000$

B. $0.005 < .625 < 0.92 < 3$

C. $0.009 < 0.100 < 0.47 < 1.125$

5. A. $0.7 = 0.70$*

B. $0.072 < 0.70$*

C. $0.70 = 0.700$

D. $0.072 < 0.107$

E. $1.7 > 0.107$

F. $0.5 > 0.072$

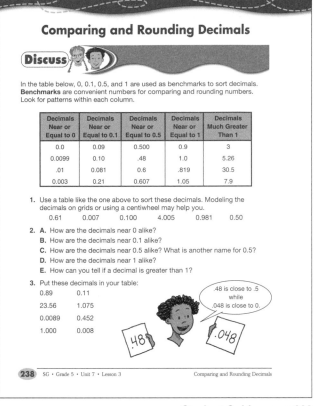

Student Guide - page 238

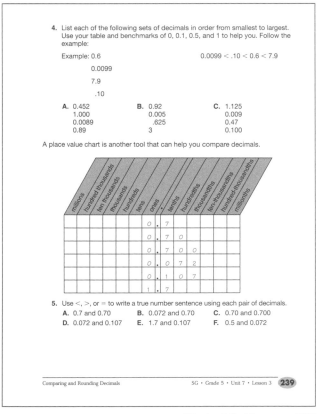

Student Guide - page 239

*Answers and/or discussion are included in the Lesson Guide.

For Questions 6–7 you may use benchmarks, decimal grids, fractions, or a place value chart to help you. Explain how you found each answer.

6. Write the following sets of decimals in order from smallest to largest:
   - **A.** 0.729   12   1.25   0.099
   - **B.** 0.8   8.0   0.888   0.08
   - **C.** 0.48   1.5   0.525   0.5

7. Use <, >, or = to write a true number sentence using each pair of decimals.
   - **A.** 0.9 and 0.900
   - **B.** 0.55 and 0.155
   - **C.** 0.23 and 0.234

Rounding Decimals

The grid at the right shows 0.892

8. **A.** Is 0.892 closer to 0.89 or 0.90?
   - **B.** Round 0.892 to the nearest hundredth.
   - **C.** Is 0.892 closer to 0.8 or 0.9?
   - **D.** Round 0.892 to the nearest tenth.
   - **E.** Is 0.892 closer to to 0 or 1?
   - **F.** Round 0.892 to the nearest whole number.

9. Round each decimal to the nearest whole number.
   - **A.** 4.32   **B.** 0.891   **C.** 19.9
   - **D.** 1.09   **E.** 35.9   **F.** 2.58

10. Round each decimal to the nearest tenth.
   - **A.** 4.32   **B.** 0.891   **C.** 0.199
   - **D.** 0.109   **E.** 0.78   **F.** 1.657

11. Round each decimal to the nearest hundredth.
   - **A.** 0.487   **B.** 0.531   **C.** 1.019
   - **D.** 0.899   **E.** 3.154   **F.** 0.607

Student Guide - page 240

Student Guide (p. 240)

6. **A.** $0.099 < 0.729 < 1.25 < 12$. Explanations will vary. Possible responses include: Using benchmarks—0.099 is close to 0, 0.729 is between $\frac{1}{2}$ and 1, 1.25 is a little greater than one, and 12 is much greater than one.*

   B. $0.08 < 0.8 < 0.888 < 8.0$. One possible explanation is: I used a place value chart and rewrote the numbers with the same number of digits, so $0.080 < 0.800 < 0.888 < 8.000$.

   C. Rewriting the numbers with the same digits gives us the following order: $0.480 < 0.500 < 0.525 < 1.500$.

7. **A.** $0.9 = 0.900$. Explanations will vary.*

   B. $0.55 > 0.155$

   C. $0.23 < 0.234$

8. **A.** Closer to 0.89

   B. 0.89

   C. Closer to 0.9

   D. 0.9

   E. Closer to 1

   F. 1

9. **A.** 4   **B.** 1
      C. 20   **D.** 1
      E. 36   **F.** 3

10. **A.** 4.3   **B.** 0.9
      C. 0.2   **D.** 0.1
      E. 0.8   **F.** 1.7

11. **A.** 0.49   **B.** 0.53
      C. 1.02   **D.** 0.90*
      E. 3.15   **F.** 0.61

*Answers and/or discussion are included in the Lesson Guide.

Student Guide (pp. 241–242)

12.

	Fraction	Decimal	Decimal to the Nearest Hundredth	Percent to the Nearest Percent
A.	$\frac{254}{1000}$	0.254	.25	25%
B.	$\frac{327}{1000}$	0.327	.33	33%
C.	$\frac{43}{1000}$	0.043	.04	4%
D.	$\frac{789}{1000}$	0.789	.79	79%
E.	$\frac{799}{1000}$	0.799	.80	80%

Homework

1. Students shade 6 grids on the *Decimal Grids* Activity Page.

2. **A.** $\frac{5}{10}$ or $\frac{1}{2}$ **B.** $\frac{87}{100}$
   C. $\frac{67}{1000}$ **D.** $\frac{2}{10}$ or $\frac{1}{5}$
   E. $\frac{20}{100}$, $\frac{2}{10}$, or $\frac{1}{5}$ **F.** $\frac{427}{1000}$

3. **A.** 50%   **B.** 20%
   C. 20%   **D.** 87%

4. **A.** 0.9   **B.** 0.1
   C. 0.4

5. **A.** 0.07   **B.** 7%

6. **A.** 0.43   **B.** 43%

7. **A.** Closer to 0.5
   B. Closer to 0.1
   C. Closer to 1
   D. Closer to 0.1

8. Explanations will vary. One possible explanation is given.
   A. 0.5 > 0.427; writing each number with the same number of digits 0.500 > 0.427
   B. 0.2 = 0.20; $\frac{2}{10} = \frac{2 \times 10}{10 \times 10} = \frac{20}{100}$
   C. 0.87 > 0.427; 8 tenths is greater than 4 tenths

9. **A.** 0.023 < 0.201 < 0.63 < 1.03 < 10
   B. 0.06 < 0.6 < 6.01 < 6.10 < 6.4
   C. 0.101 < 0.11 < 1.01 < 1.1 < 11
   D. 0.098 < 0.487 < 0.5 < 0.88 < 1.08

10. Answers will vary. Possible response: 0.37 = 0.370 and 327 thousandths is less than 370 thousandths.

12. Complete the table. The first one is done for you.

	Fraction	Decimal	Decimal (to the Nearest Hundredth)	Percent (to the Nearest Percent)
A.	$\frac{254}{1000}$	0.254	.25	25%
B.	$\frac{327}{1000}$			
C.	$\frac{43}{1000}$			
D.	$\frac{789}{1000}$			
E.	$\frac{799}{1000}$			

Use a copy of the *Decimal Grids* Activity Page to answer Questions 1–8.

1. Shade each of the following decimals. Label each one clearly.
   A. 0.5   **B.** 0.87   **C.** 0.067
   D. 0.2   **E.** 0.20   **F.** 0.427

2. Write each of the decimals in Question 1 as a common fraction.

3. **A.** Write 0.5 as a percent.
   B. Write 0.2 as a percent.
   C. Write 0.20 as a percent.
   D. Write 0.87 as a percent.

4. **A.** Round 0.87 to the nearest tenth.
   B. Round 0.067 to the nearest tenth.
   C. Round 0.427 to the nearest tenth.

5. **A.** Round 0.067 to the nearest hundredth.
   B. Write 0.067 as a percent to the nearest percent.

6. **A.** Round 0.427 to the nearest hundredth.
   B. Write 0.427 as a percent to the nearest percent.

Comparing and Rounding Decimals   SG • Grade 5 • Unit 7 • Lesson 3   **241**

Student Guide - page 241

7. **A.** Is 0.427 closer to 0.1, 0.5, or 1?
   B. Is 0.067 closer to 0.1, 0.5, or 1?
   C. Is 0.87 closer to 0.1, 0.5, or 1?
   D. Is 0.20 closer to 0.1, 0.5, or 1?

8. Use <, >, or = to write a true number sentence using each pair of decimals. Explain how you found each answer.
   A. 0.5 and 0.427   **B.** 0.2 and 0.20   **C.** 0.87 and 0.427

9. Place the following set of decimals in order from smallest to largest:
   A. 0.201   1.03   10   0.023   0.63
   B. 6.01   6.10   6.4   0.6   0.06
   C. 11   1.01   0.101   1.1   0.11
   D. 0.487   0.88   1.08   0.098   0.5

10. Look at the decimals on the blackboard in the picture. Explain how Roberto knows that 0.327 is less than 0.37.

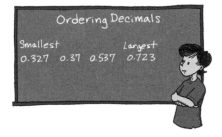

242 SG • Grade 5 • Unit 7 • Lesson 3   Comparing and Rounding Decimals

Student Guide - page 242

Name _____ Date _____

PART 3 Fractions, Decimals, and Percents

Fill in the chart, writing each number as a fraction, a decimal, and a percent. The first one is done for you. Use your centiwheel if you need to.

	Fraction	Decimal	Percent		Fraction	Decimal	Percent
A.	$\frac{1}{4}$	.25	25%	F.	$\frac{20}{100}$		
B.		.98		G.		1.00	
C.	$\frac{6}{100}$			H.	$\frac{1}{100}$		
D.			16%	I.			75%
E.		.50		J.			7%

PART 4 Adding Fractions

Solve the following problems.

A. $\frac{1}{2} + \frac{1}{4} =$ B. $\frac{1}{2} + \frac{3}{4} =$

C. $\frac{1}{2} + \frac{1}{3} =$ D. $\frac{1}{2} + \frac{2}{3} =$

E. $\frac{1}{3} + \frac{1}{4} =$ F. $\frac{2}{3} + \frac{3}{4} =$

PART 5 Reading, Writing, and Ordering Decimals

Write the following numbers as decimals and then put them in order from smallest to largest.

A. thirty-seven thousandths _____

B. two hundred forty-two and four-hundredths _____

C. one hundred nine and fourteen-thousandths _____

D. six hundred sixteen-thousandths _____

98 DAB • Grade 5 • Unit 7   DECIMALS AND PROBABILITY

Discovery Assignment Book - page 98

Name _____ Date _____

Decimals: A Closer Look

1. A. Shade 0.86.

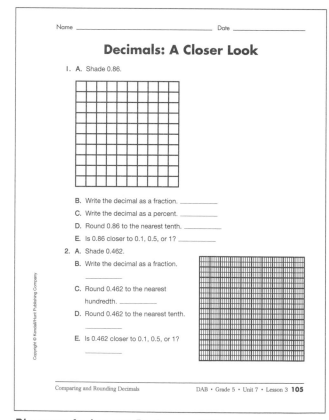

B. Write the decimal as a fraction. _____

C. Write the decimal as a percent. _____

D. Round 0.86 to the nearest tenth. _____

E. Is 0.86 closer to 0.1, 0.5, or 1? _____

2. A. Shade 0.462.

B. Write the decimal as a fraction.

_____

C. Round 0.462 to the nearest hundredth. _____

D. Round 0.462 to the nearest tenth.

_____

E. Is 0.462 closer to 0.1, 0.5, or 1?

_____

Comparing and Rounding Decimals   DAB • Grade 5 • Unit 7 • Lesson 3 **105**

Discovery Assignment Book - page 105

Discovery Assignment Book (p. 98)

Home Practice*

Part 5. Reading, Writing, and Ordering Decimals

A. .037

B. 242.04

C. 109.014

D. 0.616

   .037, 0.616, 109.014, 242.04

Discovery Assignment Book (p. 105)

Decimals: A Closer Look

1. A.   0.86

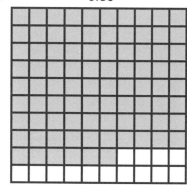

B. $\frac{86}{100}$ C. 86%

D. 0.9   E. closer to 1

2. A.*   0.462

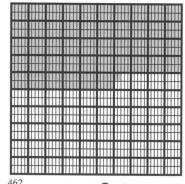

B. $\frac{462}{1000}$ C. 0.46

D. 0.5   E. closer to 0.5

*Answers for all the Home Practice in the *Discovery Assignment Book* are at the end of the unit.

Discovery Assignment Book (pp. 106–107)

3. **A.** For examples of how to shade numbers on the grids, see *Questions 1A and 2A.*

   B. 0.572

   C. 0.57

   D. 57%

4. **A.** For examples of how to shade numbers on the grids, see *Questions 1A and 2A.*

   B. 0.068

   C. 0.07

   D. 7%

5. **A.–B.** **A.** For examples of how to shade numbers on the grids, see *Questions 1A and 2A.*

   C. $\frac{3}{10}$*

   D. $\frac{30}{100}$*

   E. 30%*

   F. 30%*

   G. Yes. $\frac{3}{10} = \frac{3 \times 10}{10 \times 10} = \frac{30}{100}$ or the same area is shaded on the grids in *Questions 5A and 5B.*

   H. $0.3 = 0.30$*

6. **A.** For examples of how to shade numbers on the grids, see *Questions 1A and 2A.*

   B. $0.3 = 0.300$

   C. $0.30 = 0.300$

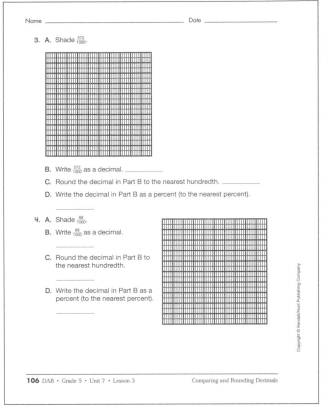

Discovery Assignment Book - page 106

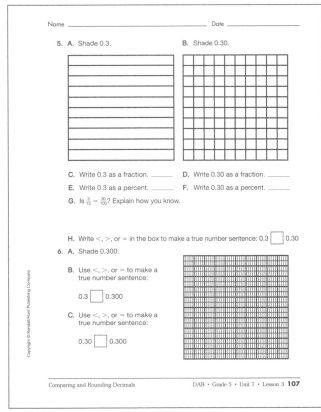

Discovery Assignment Book - page 107

*Answers and/or discussion are included in the Lesson Guide.

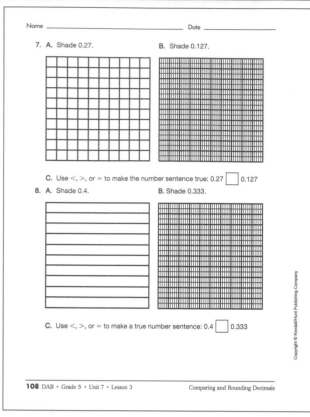

Discovery Assignment Book - page 108

Discovery Assignment Book (p. 108)

7. **A.–B.** For examples of how to shade numbers on the grids, see *Questions 1A and 2A.*

    C. $0.27 > 0.127$

8. **A.–B.** For examples of how to shade numbers on the grids, see *Questions 1A and 2A.*

    C. $0.4 > 0.333$

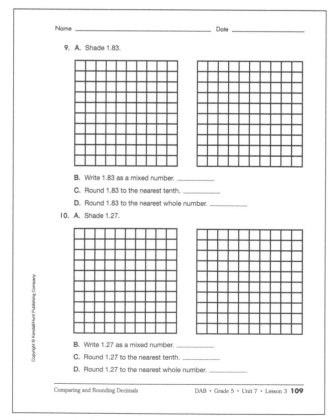

Discovery Assignment Book - page 109

Discovery Assignment Book (p. 109)

9. **A.**   1.83

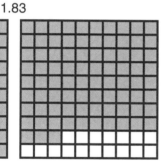

    B. $1\frac{83}{100}$

    C. 1.8

    D. 2

10. **A.** For an example of how to shade numbers on the grids, see *Question 9A.*

    B. $1\frac{27}{100}$

    C. 1.3

    D. 1

Discovery Assignment Book (p. 111)

Connect the Dots

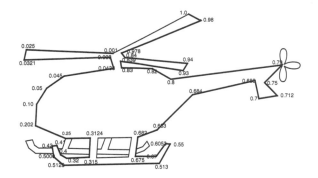

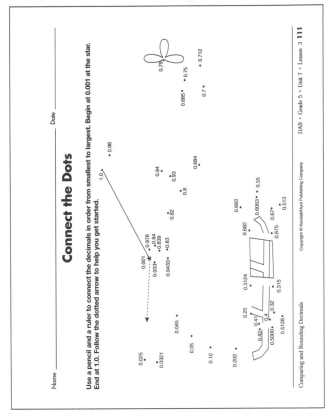

Discovery Assignment Book - page 111

Lesson 4

Adding and Subtracting Decimals

Lesson Overview

Estimated Class Sessions

1-2

In Part 1 of this lesson, students use grids in the *Discovery Assignment Book* to add and subtract decimals. Then using their *Student Guides* they learn to add and subtract decimals using paper and pencil.

Key Content

- Adding and subtracting with decimals using diagrams.
- Adding and subtracting decimals using a paper-and-pencil method.

Math Facts

DPP item K reviews math facts.

Homework

Assign *Questions 1–10* in the Homework section on the *Adding and Subtracting Decimals* Activity Pages in the *Student Guide* for homework.

Assessment

1. Use *Questions 7–8* in the Homework section on the *Adding and Subtracting Decimals* Activity Pages in the *Student Guide* as an assessment.
2. Use DPP Task L as an assessment.

Materials List

Supplies and Copies

Student	Teacher
Supplies for Each Student	**Supplies**
Copies	**Copies/Transparencies** • 1 transparency of *Adding Decimals with Grids* (*Discovery Assignment Book* Page 113) • 1 transparency of *Subtracting Decimals with Grids* (*Discovery Assignment Book* Page 117) • 1 transparency of *Decimal Place Value Chart* (*Unit Resource Guide* Page 69)

All blackline masters including assessment, transparency, and DPP masters are also on the Teacher Resource CD.

Student Books
Adding and Subtracting Decimals (*Student Guide* Pages 243–246)
Adding Decimals with Grids (*Discovery Assignment Book* Pages 113–115)
Subtracting Decimals with Grids (*Discovery Assignment Book* Pages 117–118)

Daily Practice and Problems and Home Practice
DPP items K–L (*Unit Resource Guide* Pages 22–23)

Note: Classrooms whose pacing differs significantly from the suggested pacing of the units should use the Math Facts Calendar in Section 4 of the *Facts Resource Guide* to ensure students receive the complete math facts program.

Suggestions for using the DPPs are on page 101.

K. Bit: Reviewing the Facts (URG p. 22)

Solve the given fact. Then name the other related fact or facts in the same fact family.

A. $10 \times 6 =$ B. $56 \div 7 =$

C. $45 \div 5 =$ D. $6 \times 2 =$

E. $18 \div 3 =$ F. $8 \times 4 =$

L. Task: Using the Centiwheel
(URG p. 23)

Use your centiwheel to complete the following:

1. Name a fraction that is close to 0. Give it as a common fraction, decimal, and percent.

2. Name a fraction that is just a little less than $\frac{1}{4}$. Give it as a common fraction, decimal, and percent.

3. Name a fraction that is just a little more than $\frac{1}{2}$. Give it as a common fraction, decimal, and percent.

4. Name a fraction that is close to 1. Give it as a common fraction, decimal, and percent.

Teaching the Activity

Because students are developing place value sense, do not use calculators for this lesson.

Part 1 Adding and Subtracting Decimals with Grids

Show students the area model for addition using a transparency of the *Adding Decimals with Grids* Activity Pages in the *Discovery Assignment Book.* In **Question 1,** fill in 0.4 of a hundredths grid to represent Irma's trip to the park. Then fill in another 0.4 on the same grid to represent Irma's trip back home. 0.4 mile + 0.4 mile = 0.8 mile. See Figure 22.

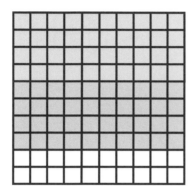

Figure 22: *Irma's bicycle trip in* **Question 1**

Irma did not meet her coach's requirements; she traveled less than one mile. Now use paper and pencil to solve the problem. Some students may notice that they could solve this problem using estimation. Since 0.4 is less than $\frac{1}{2}$, 0.4 + 0.4 is less than one.

Begin **Question 2** by estimating. Ask:

- *If Lin walks 0.25 mile and then 0.4 mile, will she walk more or less than $\frac{1}{2}$ mile?*

Students should recognize that 0.4 mile is very close to $\frac{1}{2}$ mile. So with the additional 0.25 mile, she will walk more than $\frac{1}{2}$ mile.

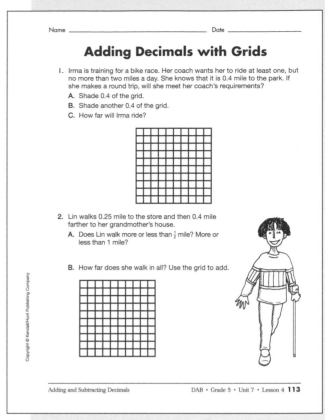

Copyright © Kendall/Hunt Publishing Company

Adding Decimals with Grids

1. Irma is training for a bike race. Her coach wants her to ride at least one, but no more than two miles a day. She knows that it is 0.4 mile to the park. If she makes a round trip, will she meet her coach's requirements?
   A. Shade 0.4 of the grid.
   B. Shade another 0.4 of the grid.
   C. How far will Irma ride?

2. Lin walks 0.25 mile to the store and then 0.4 mile farther to her grandmother's house.
   A. Does Lin walk more or less than $\frac{1}{2}$ mile? More or less than 1 mile?

   B. How far does she walk in all? Use the grid to add.

Adding and Subtracting Decimals   DAB • Grade 5 • Unit 7 • Lesson 4 **113**

Discovery Assignment Book - page 113 (Answers on p. 104)

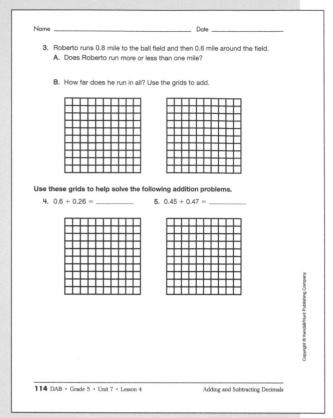

Discovery Assignment Book - page 114 (Answers on p. 105)

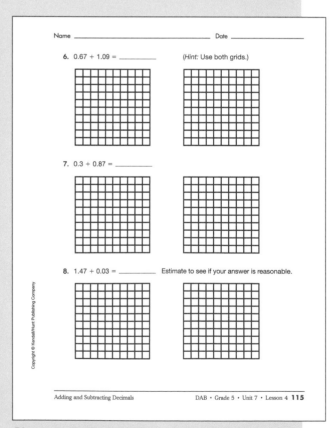

Discovery Assignment Book - page 115 (Answers on p. 105)

Ask a volunteer to set up the problem on the grid. *(Question 2B)* Then ask students to solve the problem with pencil and paper. Look for an understanding that they need to align like place values. Demonstrate how to write the problem vertically as in Figure 23.

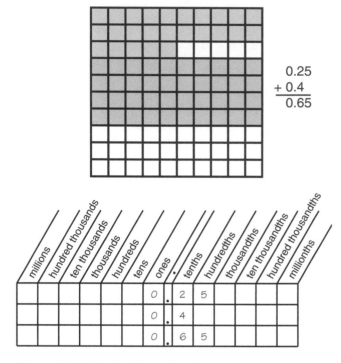

Figure 23: *Aligning like values in an addition problem*

Emphasize the need to write the problem with the tenths aligned by showing the addition on a place value chart. See Figure 23. Remind students that when they add whole numbers, they add the digits in the ones place, then the digits in the tens place, and so on. Adding decimals is the same, we just have to be careful to write the problem correctly.

Ask students to work in pairs to complete *Question 3.* They must sum 0.8 mile and 0.6 mile. *Question 3A* asks for an estimate. Since 0.8 and 0.6 are both greater than $\frac{1}{2}$, the sum is greater than one. Solving the problem with grids *(Question 3B)* shows that the sum is 1.4 miles. Using estimation and an area model helps students avoid the common mistake of reporting the sum of 0.8 and 0.6 as 0.14. Again show students how to write the problem correctly, using the place value chart if it is helpful.

Have students work through *Questions 4–8* in small groups. As you discuss the problems, talk about regrouping across a decimal. Explain that the tenths place cannot reflect more than 9 tenths. If they model *Question 7* on a grid and solve it with paper and pencil, students should see that 3 tenths + 8 tenths gives 11 tenths or 1.1, not 0.11.

The *Subtracting Decimals with Grids* Activity Pages in the *Discovery Assignment Book* follow the same procedure as the pages on addition. In **Question 1,** students fill in 0.85 on a grid, then erase 0.2 to find the solution. See Figure 24. Then they solve the problem using paper and pencil. Discuss the alignment of digits according to place value.

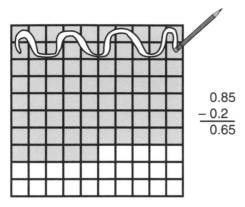

$$
\begin{array}{r}
0.85 \\
-\ 0.2 \\
\hline
0.65
\end{array}
$$

Figure 24: *Subtracting on the grids*

To complete **Question 2,** students must find the difference between 0.9 m and 0.26 m. First, they must identify the greater decimal, then shade 0.9 and erase 0.26 to find that the difference is 0.64 m. Show students how to write the problem vertically. Then ask students to explain how to solve the problem using paper and pencil. Students know that 0.9 is equivalent to 0.90, so they can rewrite the problem as 90 hundredths minus 26 hundredths as shown below.

$$
\begin{array}{r}
0.9 \\
-\ 0.26 \\
\hline
0.64
\end{array}
\qquad
\begin{array}{r}
0.90 \\
-\ 0.26 \\
\hline
0.64
\end{array}
$$

Question 3 asks students to subtract 0.95 m from 1.3 m. They will need to use two grids to solve the problem. When they solve it using paper and pencil, they will need to write 1.3 as 1.30.

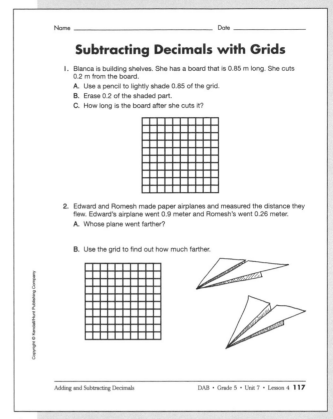

Subtracting Decimals with Grids

1. Blanca is building shelves. She has a board that is 0.85 m long. She cuts 0.2 m from the board.
   A. Use a pencil to lightly shade 0.85 of the grid.
   B. Erase 0.2 of the shaded part.
   C. How long is the board after she cuts it?

2. Edward and Romesh made paper airplanes and measured the distance they flew. Edward's airplane went 0.9 meter and Romesh's went 0.26 meter.
   A. Whose plane went farther?

   B. Use the grid to find out how much farther.

Adding and Subtracting Decimals — DAB • Grade 5 • Unit 7 • Lesson 4 **117**

Discovery Assignment Book - page 117 *(Answers on p. 106)*

3. Jerome is 1.3 m tall. His little brother is 0.95 m tall. How much taller is Jerome? Use the grids to solve the problem.

Use the grids to solve these subtraction problems.

4. 0.6 – 0.08 = _____   5. 0.95 – 0.7 = _____

6. 0.28 – 0.09 = _____   7. 0.12 – 0.08 = _____

118 DAB • Grade 5 • Unit 7 • Lesson 4 — Adding and Subtracting Decimals

Discovery Assignment Book - page 118 *(Answers on p. 106)*

Student Guide - page 243

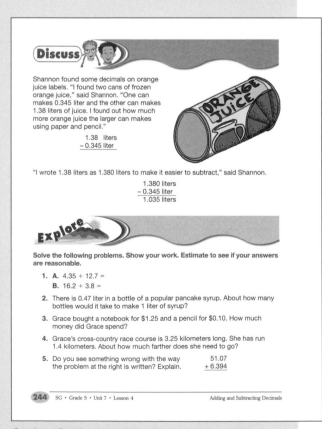

Student Guide - page 244 (Answers on p. 103)

Part 2 Adding and Subtracting Decimals with Paper and Pencil

The *Adding and Subtracting Decimals* Activity Pages in the *Student Guide* provide in-class practice to use as discussion. The vignette of Mr. Moreno's class at the grocery store reinforces the idea of aligning like places and regrouping across the decimal. It also reinforces estimation as a means to verify the reasonableness of solutions.

> **TIMS Tip**
>
> Ask students to think about Roberto and Shannon's problem using fractions or money. $\frac{1}{2}$ liter $+ \frac{1}{4}$ liter is $\frac{3}{4}$ liter. 50¢ $+$ 25¢ $=$ 75¢ or 0.75.

Ask:

- *What might Roberto have done incorrectly when adding 0.5 and 0.25 liters to get 0.30 liter?* (Roberto added the 5 in the tenths place to the 5 in the hundredths place.)

Discuss Shannon's subtraction problem. Ask:

- *Estimate the difference between 0.345 liter and 1.38 liters.* (Since 0.345 is close to 0.38, the difference is about 1.)

Shannon lines up the decimals by their correct values. She rewrites 1.38 as 1.380 so she can easily subtract 0.345. Note that Shannon's answer is close to our estimate.

Have students use paper and pencil to complete *Questions 1–9* in small groups. As students work, ask them to explain their estimation strategies.

In *Question 5,* students should see that the decimals are not aligned by their correct place values.

Questions 6–9 ask students to tell if Jessie's answers make sense. Estimation and a little mental math show that only the answer to *Question 8* is reasonable.

Questions 10–13 provide additional practice in adding and subtracting decimals. Encourage students to look at their answers to see if they make sense.

> **Journal Prompt**
>
> Why did the mouse in the *Student Guide* say "You're all out of line?"

Math Facts

DPP Bit K reviews the multiplication and division facts.

Homework and Practice

Homework *Questions 1–10* in the *Student Guide* provide mixed addition and subtraction practice.

Assessment

- Use Homework *Questions 7–8* in the *Student Guide* as an assessment.
- Use DPP item L to assess students' understanding of fractions, decimals, and percents. Students will need centiwheels.

Jessie solved the following problems. Use estimates to tell if each answer is reasonable. Explain your reasoning.

6. .8 + .7 = .15
7. 12.8 + 6.7 = 73.8
8. 15.002 + 2.5 = 17.117
9. 3.706 − 1.597 = .2289

Solve.

10.	11.	12.	13.
0.124 + 2.33	1.49 − 1.08	3.1 + 0.13	0.379 + 0.375

Homework

Use paper and pencil to solve the problems. For some problems you will need an exact answer. For other problems, an estimate will do.

1. There are 15.1 servings in a box of a popular cereal. How many servings are in two boxes?

2. If we use the serving information on the label of a bottle of barbecue sauce, there are 25.6 servings per bottle. About how many servings are in three bottles?

3. One serving of a very well-known tortilla chip has 27.6 grams. How many grams are in two servings?

4. The same bag of tortilla chips has a total of 382.7 grams. About how many grams will be left after the two servings from Question 3 are eaten?

Adding and Subtracting Decimals   SG • Grade 5 • Unit 7 • Lesson 4   **245**

Student Guide - page 245 (Answers on p. 103)

---

5. A portion of whole wheat flour contains 30.2 grams. A recipe calls for 2 portions. How many grams are in two portions?

6. A small bag of whole wheat flour contains 907 grams. How much is left after the two portions from Question 5 are used?

7. Use estimates to tell which of the following solutions are reasonable.
   A. 0.6 + 0.06 = 0.12
   B. 1.78 − .99 = .79
   C. 0.07 + 0.004 = 0.074

8. Solve. Estimate to check if your answers are reasonable.
   A. 80.23 + 22.58 =
   B. 13.89 − 5.53 =
   C. 17.7 + 8.62 =
   D. 0.64 + 0.9 =
   E. 1.3 + 0.687 =
   F. 42.34 + 87.9 =

9. Tanya wanted to buy a $5.00 binder for her notes. She has saved $3.60 so far. How much more money does Tanya need to save?

10. Linda and Jackie pooled their money to buy some snacks. They had $9.57 altogether. If Jackie gave $4.65, how much money did Linda give?

246   SG • Grade 5 • Unit 7 • Lesson 4   Adding and Subtracting Decimals

Student Guide - page 246 (Answers on p. 104)

At a Glance

Math Facts and Daily Practice and Problems

DPP item K reviews math facts. Task L provides practice with fractions, decimals, and percents with centiwheels.

Part 1. Adding and Subtracting Decimals with Grids

1. Use the *Adding Decimals with Grids* Activity Pages in the *Discovery Assignment Book* to develop students' understanding of the procedures for adding decimals.
2. Use the *Subtracting Decimals with Grids* Activity Pages in the *Discovery Assignment Book* to develop understanding of procedures for subtracting decimals.

Part 2. Adding and Subtracting Decimals with Paper and Pencil

Students complete *Questions 1–13* on the *Adding and Subtracting Decimals* Activity Pages in the Student Guide for in-class discussion.

Homework

Assign *Questions 1–10* in the Homework section on the *Adding and Subtracting Decimals* Activity Pages in the *Student Guide* for homework.

Assessment

1. Use *Questions 7–8* in the Homework section on the *Adding and Subtracting Decimals* Activity Pages in the *Student Guide* as an assessment.
2. Use DPP Task L as an assessment.

Answer Key is on pages 103–106.

Notes:

Student Guide (p. 244)

1. **A.** 17.05
   B. 20
2. about 2
3. $1.35
4. 1.85 km
5. Like place values need to be aligned. The 0 in the tenths place needs to be aligned with the 3, which is also in the tenths place.

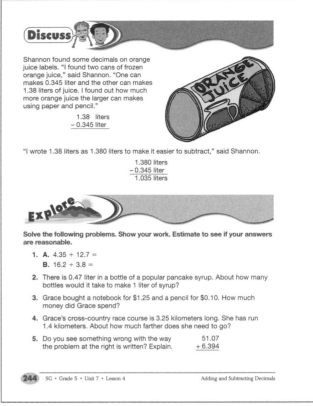

Student Guide - page 244

Student Guide (p. 245)

6. The answer is not reasonable. Both .8 and .7 are close to 1. Therefore the answer should be close to 2.

7. The answer is not reasonable; 12.8 is close to 13 and 6.7 is close to 7. Therefore the answer should be close to 20.

8. The answer is reasonable; 15.002 is close to 15 and 2.5 is close to 2. Therefore the answer should be close to 17 and it is.

9. The answer is not reasonable; 3.706 is close to 4 and 1.597 is close to 2. Therefore the answer should be close to 2.

10. 2.454
11. 0.41
12. 3.23
13. 0.754

Homework

1. 30.2 servings
2. Answers will vary. One possible answer is about 75 servings.
3. 55.2 grams
4. Answers will vary. One possible answer is 380 g – 50 g = 330 g.

Student Guide - page 245

5. A portion of whole wheat flour contains 30.2 grams. A recipe calls for 2 portions. How many grams are in two portions?

6. A small bag of whole wheat flour contains 907 grams. How much is left after the two portions from Question 5 are used?

7. Use estimates to tell which of the following solutions are reasonable.
   A. 0.6 + 0.06 = 0.12
   B. 1.78 − .99 = .79
   C. 0.07 + 0.004 = 0.074

8. Solve. Estimate to check if your answers are reasonable.
   A. 80.23 + 22.58 =
   B. 13.89 − 5.53 =
   C. 17.7 + 8.62 =
   D. 0.64 + 0.9 =
   E. 1.3 + 0.687 =
   F. 42.34 + 87.9 =

9. Tanya wanted to buy a $5.00 binder for her notes. She has saved $3.60 so far. How much more money does Tanya need to save?

10. Linda and Jackie pooled their money to buy some snacks. They had $9.57 altogether. If Jackie gave $4.65, how much money did Linda give?

Student Guide - page 246

Student Guide (p. 246)

5. 60.4 grams

6. 846.6 grams

7. **A.** Not reasonable; 0.06 is close to 0.1. Therefore the answer should be close to 0.7.

   B. Reasonable.

   C. Reasonable.

8. **A.** 102.81

   B. 8.36

   C. 26.32

   D. 1.54

   E. 1.987

   F. 130.24

9. $1.40

10. $4.92

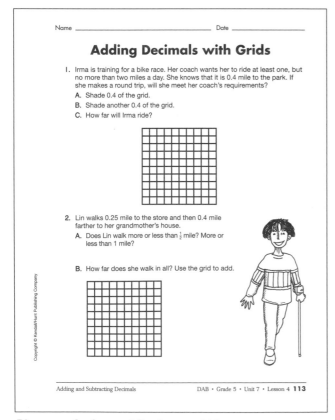

Copyright © Kendall/Hunt Publishing Company

Name _____ Date _____

Adding Decimals with Grids

1. Irma is training for a bike race. Her coach wants her to ride at least one, but no more than two miles a day. She knows that it is 0.4 mile to the park. If she makes a round trip, will she meet her coach's requirements?
   A. Shade 0.4 of the grid.
   B. Shade another 0.4 of the grid.
   C. How far will Irma ride?

2. Lin walks 0.25 mile to the store and then 0.4 mile farther to her grandmother's house.
   A. Does Lin walk more or less than ½ mile? More or less than 1 mile?

   B. How far does she walk in all? Use the grid to add.

Discovery Assignment Book - page 113

Discovery Assignment Book (p. 113)

Adding Decimals with Grids

1.*Irma will not meet her coach's requirements.

   A.–B. See Figure 22 in Lesson Guide 4.

   C. 0.8 miles

2. **A.** More than ½ mile. Less than 1 mile.*

   B. 0.65 miles. See Figure 23 in Lesson Guide 4.

*Answers and/or discussion are included in the Lesson Guide.

Discovery Assignment Book (p. 114)

3.* **A.** More than 1 mile.

B. 1.4 miles

1.4

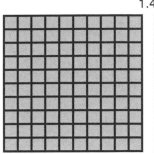 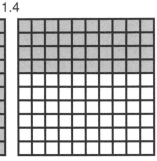

4. 0.86

5. .92

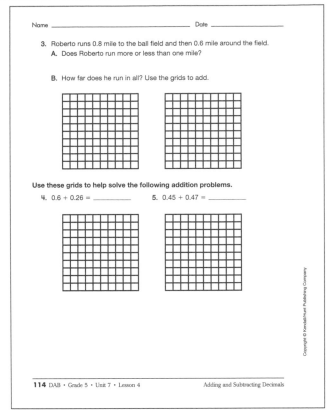

Discovery Assignment Book - page 114

Discovery Assignment Book (p. 115)

6. 1.76

7. 1.17*

8. 1.5

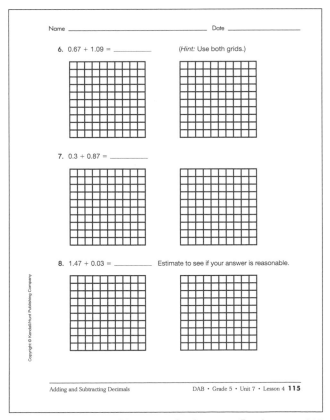

Discovery Assignment Book - page 115

*Answers and/or discussion are included in the Lesson Guide.

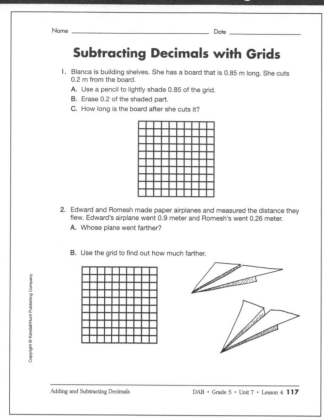

Name _____ Date _____

Subtracting Decimals with Grids

1. Blanca is building shelves. She has a board that is 0.85 m long. She cuts 0.2 m from the board.
   A. Use a pencil to lightly shade 0.85 of the grid.
   B. Erase 0.2 of the shaded part.
   C. How long is the board after she cuts it?

2. Edward and Romesh made paper airplanes and measured the distance they flew. Edward's airplane went 0.9 meter and Romesh's went 0.26 meter.
   A. Whose plane went farther?

   B. Use the grid to find out how much farther.

Adding and Subtracting Decimals   DAB • Grade 5 • Unit 7 • Lesson 4 **117**

Discovery Assignment Book - page 117

Discovery Assignment Book (p. 117)

Subtracting Decimals with Grids

1. **A.–B.*** See Figure 24 in Lesson Guide 4.
   C. 0.65 m
2.* **A.** Edward's
   B. 0.64 meters

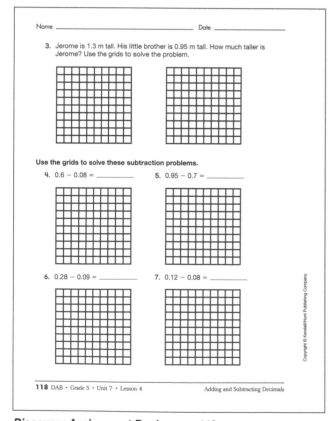

Name _____ Date _____

3. Jerome is 1.3 m tall. His little brother is 0.95 m tall. How much taller is Jerome? Use the grids to solve the problem.

Use the grids to solve these subtraction problems.

4. 0.6 − 0.08 = _____   5. 0.95 − 0.7 = _____

6. 0.28 − 0.09 = _____   7. 0.12 − 0.08 = _____

118 DAB • Grade 5 • Unit 7 • Lesson 4   Adding and Subtracting Decimals

Discovery Assignment Book - page 118

Discovery Assignment Book (p. 118)

3. 0.35 m*

0.35

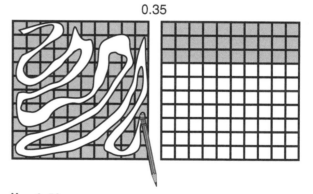

4. 0.52
5. 0.25
6. .19
7. 0.04

---

*Answers and/or discussion are included in the Lesson Guide.

Lesson 5

Multiplying Decimals with Area

Lesson Overview

Estimated Class Sessions
1-2

Students solve problems involving multiplication of decimals using paper and pencil. They use two methods to place the decimal point in the product. They can either estimate the products or model the multiplication by finding the area of rectangles on grid paper.

Key Content

- Multiplying decimals using an area model.

Homework

1. Assign the Homework section in the *Multiplying Decimals with Area* Activity Pages in the *Student Guide*.
2. Assign Part 6 of the Home Practice.

Curriculum Sequence

Before This Unit

Students reviewed paper-and-pencil multiplication methods in Unit 2. Students drew rectangles on grids to multiply in Unit 4 Lesson 1.

After This Unit

Students will look at different multiplication methods in Unit 9. They will use multiplication of decimals to solve problems in later units. For example, students multiply decimals to find the circumference of circles in Unit 14.

Materials List

Supplies and Copies

Student	Teacher
Supplies for Each Student • ruler	**Supplies**
Copies • 1–3 copies of *Centimeter Grid Paper* per student (*Unit Resource Guide* Page 113)	**Copies/Transparencies** • 1 transparency of *Centimeter Grid Paper* (*Unit Resource Guide* Page 113)

All blackline masters including assessment, transparency, and DPP masters are also on the Teacher Resource CD.

Student Books

Multiplying Decimals with Area (*Student Guide* Pages 247–251)

Daily Practice and Problems and Home Practice

DPP items M–N (*Unit Resource Guide* Page 23)
Home Practice Part 6 (*Discovery Assignment Book* Page 99)

Note: Classrooms whose pacing differs significantly from the suggested pacing of the units should use the Math Facts Calendar in Section 4 of the *Facts Resource Guide* to ensure students receive the complete math facts program.

Daily Practice and Problems

Suggestions for using the DPPs are on page 111.

M. Bit: Ordering Decimals (URG p. 23)

Put the following sets of numbers in order from smallest to largest.

A. $2\frac{3}{4}$, 2.5, 2.0, 0.2

B. 4.5, $4\frac{1}{4}$, 0.4, $4\frac{1}{5}$, 4

C. 71, 7.1, 710, 0.7, 710.1, $71\frac{1}{2}$

N. Challenge: The Important Point
 (URG p. 23)

Place a decimal point in the following numbers so the four numbers will increase in order from left to right. Read the numbers to a friend.

30274   30269   29145   14058

Try to do this in more than one way.

Have students read the vignette on the *Multiplying Decimals with Area* Activity Pages in the *Student Guide.* Jacob, Jackie, Jerome, and John estimate how much carpet Mr. Moreno needs for his front hall, which measures 8.5 ft × 7.5 ft. Discuss the convenient numbers the students use to make their estimates. Jacob rounds up to 9 ft and 8 ft. Since both 9 ft and 8 ft are larger than the actual dimensions of the hall, Jacob's estimate is too high. Jackie's convenient numbers are less than the actual dimensions of the room, so her estimate is too low. Jerome's estimate is probably the closest, since one of his convenient numbers is lower and the other is higher than the actual dimensions.

To find the actual amount of carpet needed, John drew an 8.5 by 7.5 rectangle on grid paper. Students previously worked with multiplying whole numbers using an area model. Extend this model to decimals. Shade a rectangle that has dimensions of 8.5 × 7.5 units on a transparency of *Centimeter Grid Paper.* The amount shaded is the area or the product of the multiplication. In **Question 1,** students can multiply 8 × 7 to find the number of whole squares. They can piece together the remaining fractional parts of squares to find a total shaded area of 63.75 square feet as shown in Figure 25.

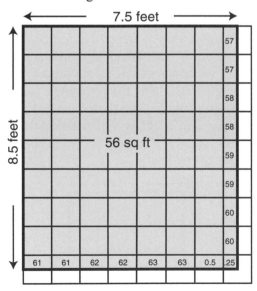

Figure 25: *Finding the area of a room that measures 8.5 ft by 7.5 ft*

Multiplying Decimals with Area

Discuss

Mr. Moreno decided to carpet his front hall. His front hall measures 8.5 feet by 7.5 feet. Mr. Moreno challenged his students to find out how many square feet of carpet he needs to buy.

"I can estimate the area for you, Mr. Moreno," said Jacob. "8.5 feet is about 9 feet and 7.5 feet is about 8 feet. 9 feet × 8 feet = 72 square feet of carpet."

"Jacob, you estimated too high. You'll have too much carpet," said Jackie. "I think a better estimate is 8 feet × 7 feet = 56 square feet of carpet."

"Jackie, you estimated too low. You won't have enough carpet," said Jerome. "I think the best estimate is to round 8.5 feet down to 8 feet and 7.5 feet up to 8 feet. 8 feet × 8 feet = 64 square feet of carpet."

"Those estimates are useful, but I need a more exact answer to buy carpet," said Mr. Moreno.

Multiplying Decimals with Area   SG • Grade 5 • Unit 7 • Lesson 5   **247**

Student Guide - page 247

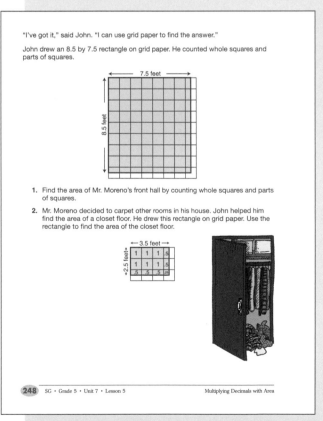

"I've got it," said John. "I can use grid paper to find the answer."

John drew an 8.5 by 7.5 rectangle on grid paper. He counted whole squares and parts of squares.

1. Find the area of Mr. Moreno's front hall by counting whole squares and parts of squares.

2. Mr. Moreno decided to carpet other rooms in his house. John helped him find the area of a closet floor. He drew this rectangle on grid paper. Use the rectangle to find the area of the closet floor.

248 SG • Grade 5 • Unit 7 • Lesson 5   Multiplying Decimals with Area

Student Guide - page 248 (Answers on p. 114)

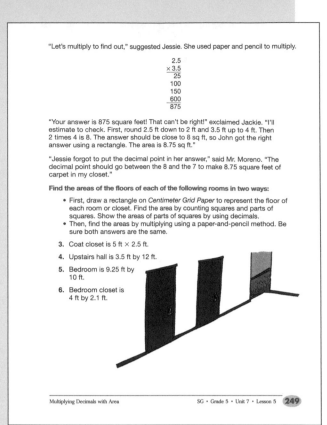

Student Guide - page 249 *(Answers on p. 114)*

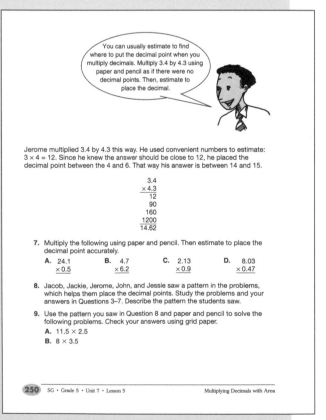

Student Guide - page 250 *(Answers on p. 115)*

In **Question 2,** John uses a rectangle on grid paper to find the area of the floor of a closet that is 2.5 ft by 3.5 ft. John's rectangle is shown in the *Student Guide* and students use it to find the area of the closet: 8.75 sq ft.

Jessie uses the all-partials method to multiply 2.5 × 3.5. Since she does not know where to put the decimal point, her answer is 875. By estimating the product to be about 8 sq ft, students can place the decimal correctly. They know they are correct, because the answer matches what John found when he used the area model.

> ## Content Note
>
>
> **Multiplying Decimals.** Although we previously stressed using place value, if using a paper-and-pencil method to multiply numbers involving decimals, it is best to multiply the numbers as whole numbers first. Then students can estimate where the decimal point will go and insert it.

To complete **Questions 3–6,** students multiply decimals in two ways. First they draw rectangles on *Centimeter Grid Paper* and find the areas of rectangles. Then they multiply using a paper-and-pencil method and place the decimal based on the area of their rectangles. Encourage students to use rulers to carefully draw their rectangles for **Questions 5–6.**

To complete **Question 6,** since 1 cm represents 1 foot on *Centimeter Grid Paper,* students can measure the width of the rectangle with a centimeter ruler as shown in Figure 26. Using the rectangles, they can see that the area covered by whole squares is 8 feet. Then they can skip count by tenths to find the area of the partial squares. The total area of the closet is 8.4 sq ft.

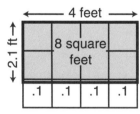

Figure 26: *2.1 × 4*

Question 7 asks students to use paper and pencil to multiply decimals. They place the decimal point by estimating the product. Discuss students' estimation strategies. To estimate the product of 24.1 × 0.5 in *Question 7A,* students can find $\frac{1}{2}$ of 24 or $\frac{1}{2}$ of 20. Using either strategy, they should be able to place the decimal properly so that the answer is close to 10 or 12.

$$
\begin{array}{r}
24.1 \\
\times\ 0.5 \\
\hline
5 \\
200 \\
1000 \\
\hline
12.05
\end{array}
$$

Question 8 encourages students to look for a pattern in the problems solved in *Questions 3–7* that will help them place the decimal. To describe the pattern, students may say, "The sum of the number of digits after the decimal points in the factors should equal the number of digits after the decimal point in the product." Encourage students to continue estimating as they begin to apply the pattern when they multiply decimals.

Homework and Practice

- Assign the Homework section of the *Multiplying Decimals with Area* Activity Pages in the *Student Guide.*

- Use DPP items M and N to improve students' number sense with decimals.

- Assign Part 6 of the Home Practice, which includes operations with decimals.

Answers for Part 6 of the Home Practice are in the Answer Key at the end of this lesson and at the end of this unit.

Homework

Estimate the answers to the following problems. Then use paper and pencil to multiply. Use your estimates to place the decimal point in the answer.

1. 4.21 ×5.0	2. 42.1 ×0.9	3. 4.21 ×0.5	4. 23.9 ×1.0
5. 2.39 ×0.5	6. 2.39 ×0.7	7. 53 ×1.6	8. 0.53 ×0.8
9. 0.53 ×1.6	10. 25 ×2.4	11. 2.5 ×0.2	12. 0.25 ×0.4

13. Mr. Moreno is buying sports equipment for the school. He bought three basketballs and paid $19.79 for each one. How much money did he spend on basketballs?

14. The school owns 3 ping-pong tables, but the paddles and balls are lost. He can buy a set of six balls, four paddles, and one net for $29.29. How much will it cost for Mr. Moreno to buy one set for each table?

15. Mr. Moreno wants to help his class become physically fit. He decides to buy 4 jump ropes. The ropes are $15.65 each. How much do 4 ropes cost?

16. In order for his class to play softball, he needs 3 bats, 2 balls, and a set of bases. Each set of bases includes first, second, third, home plate, and a pitcher's mound. The bats are $14.55 each. The balls are $4.55 each. Each of the bases costs $2.59. How much money will he spend on softball equipment?

Multiplying Decimals with Area   SG • Grade 5 • Unit 7 • Lesson 5   **251**

Student Guide - page 251 (Answers on p. 115)

Name _____   Date _____

PART 6 Working with Decimals
Solve the following problems using paper and pencil. Estimate to be sure your answers are reasonable.

A. 45.6 + 12.35 =   B. 0.76 + 0.043 =   C. 0.89 × 4 =

D. 7.3 − 0.53 =   E. 4.8 × 8.3 =   F. 0.67 × 2 =

G. 176.4 + 0.385 =   H. 456.07 − 128.43 =   I. 4.577 × 0.5 =

PART 7 What's the Chance?
Manny works at the miniature golf range. The owner bought 20 new balls. He bought 5 red balls, 2 white balls, 3 green balls, 7 orange balls, and 3 yellow balls. Manny put all the new balls in a bucket. In between customers, he tries a probability experiment. If Manny picks one ball, the probability that he will pick a yellow ball is $\frac{3}{20}$.

1. Without looking, he picks one ball from the bucket. Write each of the following probabilities as a fraction, decimal, and percent:
   A. The probability that he will pick a red ball.
   B. The probability that he will pick a white ball.
   C. The probability that he will pick a green ball.
   D. The probability that he will pick an orange ball.

2. What color ball will Manny most likely pick? Justify your answer.

3. Manny predicts that he will choose a red ball or an orange ball. Is this a good prediction? Why or why not?

DECIMALS AND PROBABILITY   DAB • Grade 5 • Unit 7   **99**

Discovery Assignment Book - page 99 (Answers on p. 116)

Math Facts and Daily Practice and Problems

DPP items M and N develop number sense with decimals.

Teaching the Activity

1. Students read the vignette on the *Multiplying Decimals with Area* Activity Pages in the *Student Guide*.
2. Discuss Jacob's, Jackie's, and Jerome's estimates.
3. Students multiply decimals by using an area model and paper and pencil. *(Questions 1–2)*
4. Students solve multiplication of decimal problems in two ways. They find the area of rectangles on grid paper and use the results to place the decimal point in the product when they solve the same problem using a paper-and-pencil method. *(Questions 3–6)*
5. Students use a paper-and-pencil method to multiply decimals. They estimate the answers to determine appropriate placement of the decimal point. *(Question 7)*
6. Students look for patterns in the problems in *Questions 3–7* that will help them place the decimal point when they multiply decimals using paper and pencil. *(Questions 8–9)*

Homework

1. Assign the Homework section in the *Multiplying Decimals with Area* Activity Pages in the *Student Guide*.
2. Assign Part 6 of the Home Practice.

Answer Key is on pages 114–116.

Notes:

Centimeter Grid Paper

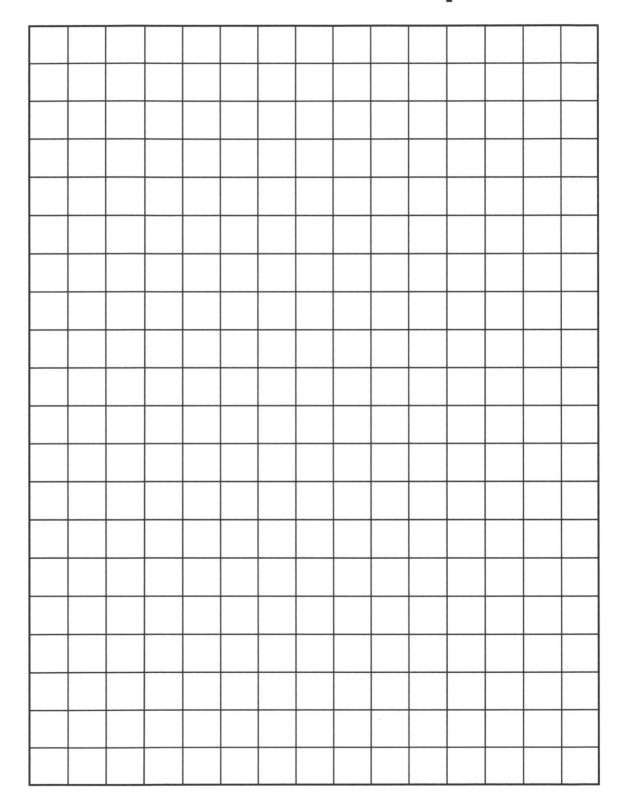

"I've got it," said John. "I can use grid paper to find the answer."

John drew an 8.5 by 7.5 rectangle on grid paper. He counted whole squares and parts of squares.

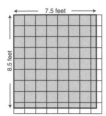

1. Find the area of Mr. Moreno's front hall by counting whole squares and parts of squares.

2. Mr. Moreno decided to carpet other rooms in his house. John helped him find the area of a closet floor. He drew this rectangle on grid paper. Use the rectangle to find the area of the closet floor.

Student Guide - page 248

Student Guide (p. 248)

1. See Figure 25 in Lesson Guide 5. 63.75 square feet.*

2. 8.75 square feet*

"Let's multiply to find out," suggested Jessie. She used paper and pencil to multiply.

$$\begin{array}{r} 2.5 \\ \times 3.5 \\ \hline 25 \\ 100 \\ 150 \\ 600 \\ \hline 875 \end{array}$$

"Your answer is 875 square feet! That can't be right!" exclaimed Jackie. "I'll estimate to check. First, round 2.5 down to 2 ft and 3.5 up to 4 ft. Then 2 times 4 is 8. The answer should be close to 8 sq ft, so John got the right answer using a rectangle. The area is 8.75 sq ft."

"Jessie forgot to put the decimal point in her answer," said Mr. Moreno. "The decimal point should go between the 8 and the 7 to make 8.75 square feet of carpet in my closet."

Find the areas of the floors of each of the following rooms in two ways:

- First, draw a rectangle on *Centimeter Grid Paper* to represent the floor of each room or closet. Find the area by counting squares and parts of squares. Show the areas of parts of squares by using decimals.
- Then, find the areas by multiplying using a paper-and-pencil method. Be sure both answers are the same.

3. Coat closet is 5 ft × 2.5 ft.

4. Upstairs hall is 3.5 ft by 12 ft.

5. Bedroom is 9.25 ft by 10 ft.

6. Bedroom closet is 4 ft by 2.1 ft.

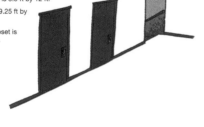

Student Guide - page 249

Student Guide (p. 249)

3. 12.5 sq ft

4. 42 sq ft

5. 92.5 sq ft

6. 8.4 sq ft. See Figure 26 in Lesson Guide 5.*

---

*Answers and/or discussion are included in the Lesson Guide.

Student Guide (p. 250)

7. **A.** 12.05*
   B. 29.14
   C. 1.917
   D. 3.7741

8. The number of decimal places in the product equals the total number of decimal places in the numbers multiplied.*

9. **A.** 28.75
   B. 28

You can usually estimate to find where to put the decimal point when you multiply decimals. Multiply 3.4 by 4.3 using paper and pencil as if there were no decimal points. Then, estimate to place the decimal.

Jerome multiplied 3.4 by 4.3 this way. He used convenient numbers to estimate: $3 \times 4 = 12$. Since he knew the answer should be close to 12, he placed the decimal point between the 4 and 6. That way his answer is between 14 and 15.

$$\begin{array}{r} 3.4 \\ \times 4.3 \\ \hline 12 \\ 90 \\ 160 \\ 1200 \\ \hline 14.62 \end{array}$$

7. Multiply the following using paper and pencil. Then estimate to place the decimal point accurately.

   A. 24.1
   $\times 0.5$
   B. 4.7
   $\times 6.2$
   C. 2.13
   $\times 0.9$
   D. 8.03
   $\times 0.47$

8. Jacob, Jackie, Jerome, John, and Jessie saw a pattern in the problems, which helps them place the decimal points. Study the problems and your answers in Questions 3–7. Describe the pattern the students saw.

9. Use the pattern you saw in Question 8 and paper and pencil to solve the following problems. Check your answers using grid paper.
   A. 11.5×2.5
   B. 8×3.5

250 SG • Grade 5 • Unit 7 • Lesson 5   Multiplying Decimals with Area

Student Guide - page 250

Student Guide (p. 251)

Homework

1. 21.05
2. 37.89
3. 2.105
4. 23.9
5. 1.195
6. 1.673
7. 84.8
8. 0.424
9. 0.848
10. 60
11. 0.5
12. 0.1
13. $59.37
14. $87.87
15. 62.60
16. $65.70

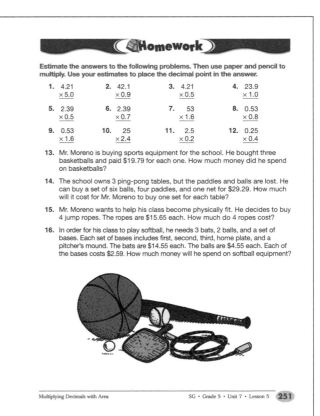

Homework

Estimate the answers to the following problems. Then use paper and pencil to multiply. Use your estimates to place the decimal point in the answer.

1. 4.21 $\times 5.0$
2. 42.1 $\times 0.9$
3. 4.21 $\times 0.5$
4. 23.9 $\times 1.0$
5. 2.39 $\times 0.5$
6. 2.39 $\times 0.7$
7. 53 $\times 1.6$
8. 0.53 $\times 0.8$
9. 0.53 $\times 1.6$
10. 25 $\times 2.4$
11. 2.5 $\times 0.2$
12. 0.25 $\times 0.4$

13. Mr. Moreno is buying sports equipment for the school. He bought three basketballs and paid $19.79 for each one. How much money did he spend on basketballs?

14. The school owns 3 ping-pong tables, but the paddles and balls are lost. He can buy a set of six balls, four paddles, and one net for $29.29. How much will it cost for Mr. Moreno to buy one set for each table?

15. Mr. Moreno wants to help his class become physically fit. He decides to buy 4 jump ropes. The ropes are $15.65 each. How much do 4 ropes cost?

16. In order for his class to play softball, he needs 3 bats, 2 balls, and a set of bases. Each set of bases includes first, second, third, home plate, and a pitcher's mound. The bats are $14.55 each. The balls are $4.55 each. Each of the bases costs $2.59. How much money will he spend on softball equipment?

Multiplying Decimals with Area   SG • Grade 5 • Unit 7 • Lesson 5 **251**

Student Guide - page 251

*Answers and/or discussion are included in the Lesson Guide.

Name _____ Date _____

PART 6 Working with Decimals

Solve the following problems using paper and pencil. Estimate to be sure your answers are reasonable.

A. $45.6 + 12.35 =$ B. $0.76 + 0.043 =$ C. $0.89 \times 4 =$

D. $7.3 - 0.53 =$ E. $4.8 \times 8.3 =$ F. $0.67 \times 2 =$

G. $176.4 + 0.385 =$ H. $456.07 - 128.43 =$ I. $4.577 \times 0.5 =$

PART 7 What's the Chance?

Manny works at the miniature golf range. The owner bought 20 new balls. He bought 5 red balls, 2 white balls, 3 green balls, 7 orange balls, and 3 yellow balls. Manny put all the new balls in a bucket. In between customers, he tries a probability experiment. If Manny picks one ball, the probability that he will pick a yellow ball is $\frac{3}{20}$.

1. Without looking, he picks one ball from the bucket. Write each of the following probabilities as a fraction, decimal, and percent:
   A. The probability that he will pick a red ball.
   B. The probability that he will pick a white ball.
   C. The probability that he will pick a green ball.
   D. The probability that he will pick an orange ball.

2. What color ball will Manny most likely pick? Justify your answer.

3. Manny predicts that he will choose a red ball or an orange ball. Is this a good prediction? Why or why not?

DECIMALS AND PROBABILITY   DAB • Grade 5 • Unit 7   **99**

Discovery Assignment Book - page 99

Discovery Assignment Book (p. 99)

Home Practice*

Part 6. Working with Decimals

A. 57.95

B. 0.803

C. 3.56

D. 6.77

E. 39.84

F. 1.34

G. 176.785

H. 327.64

I. 2.2885

*Answers for all the Home Practice in the *Discovery Assignment Book* are at the end of the unit.

Paper-and-Pencil Decimal Multiplication

Lesson Overview

Students use paper and pencil to multiply decimals. They learn to place decimal points in products.

Key Content

- Multiplying decimals using a paper-and-pencil method.

Math Facts

DPP Bit O reviews the multiplication and division facts.

Homework

Assign the Homework section in the *Student Guide*.

Assessment

Use the *Decimal Quiz* as an assessment of students' skills.

Materials List

Supplies and Copies

Student	Teacher
Supplies for Each Student	**Supplies**
Copies • 1 copy of *Decimal Quiz* per student (*Unit Resource Guide* Page 123)	**Copies/Transparencies**

All blackline masters including assessment, transparency, and DPP masters are also on the Teacher Resource CD.

Student Books

Paper-and-Pencil Decimal Multiplication (*Student Guide* Pages 252–254)

Daily Practice and Problems and Home Practice

DPP items O–P (*Unit Resource Guide* Page 24)

Note: Classrooms whose pacing differs significantly from the suggested pacing of the units should use the Math Facts Calendar in Section 4 of the *Facts Resource Guide* to ensure students receive the complete math facts program.

Daily Practice and Problems

Suggestions for using the DPPs are on page 121.

O. Bit: Reviewing the Facts (URG p. 24)

Solve the given fact. Then name the other related fact or facts in the same fact family.

A. $24 \div 4 =$ B. $5 \times 5 =$

C. $70 \div 10 =$ D. $18 \div 9 =$

E. $7 \times 6 =$ F. $15 \div 3 =$

P. Task: Sums and Differences (URG p. 24)

Estimate to answer the following. Do not use paper and pencil.

1. Is $3.694 + 4.076$ closer to 7 or 8? How do you know?

2. Is $5 - 3.7$ more or less than 2? How do you know?

3. Is $1.355 + 9.207$ more or less than 10.5? How do you know?

4. Is $14.342 - 0.018$ more or less than 14? How do you know?

5. Is $13.9 + 1.012$ more or less than 15? How do you know?

Student Guide - page 252

Student Guide - page 253 *(Answers on p. 124)*

In Lesson 5, students learned to estimate the product of two factors with decimals. Using these estimates, they solved multiplication problems and placed the decimal point appropriately. After solving several problems, they looked for a pattern to help them place decimal points in products. Review the homework from Lesson 5. Ask students to look at the problems to see if the pattern holds for the homework problems.

Teaching the Activity

Review the rule for placing decimal points in products by reading the *Paper-and-Pencil Decimal Multiplication* Activity Pages in the *Student Guide.*

Question 1 asks students to state the rule in their own words. They must explain how to use it on a sample problem and correctly place the decimal.

Examine the factors in *Questions 2–5.* Ask students how many digits will come after the decimal point in the products for each question. Then have students solve the problems and place the decimal point using estimation and the rule.

Discuss *Question 4* with students ($0.8 \times .003 = 0.0024$). Be sure students write zeros in the tenths and hundredths places of the product so there will be a total of 4 digits to the right of the decimal.

> ## TIMS Tip
>
> As a class, compare procedures for adding and subtracting decimals to procedures for multiplying decimals. Using examples, remind students that to add (and subtract) they need to add or subtract like places by lining up the decimals. However, to multiply decimals it is not necessary to line up the decimals in the problem. The decimal point is placed in the product after the calculations are complete.

Math Facts

DPP item O reviews the multiplication and division facts.

Homework and Practice

- Assign the Homework section of the *Paper-and-Pencil Decimal Multiplication* Activity Pages in the *Student Guide.*

- Use DPP item P to practice estimating sums and differences of decimals.

Assessment

Use the *Decimal Quiz* Assessment Page to assess students' skills in ordering, rounding, adding, subtracting, and multiplying decimals.

Solve the following problems. Estimate to check and see if your answers are reasonable.

1. A cheeseburger from a popular fast-food restaurant has 5.7 grams of saturated fat. If you eat $2\frac{1}{2}$ cheeseburgers, how much saturated fat will you eat?

2. A bottle of liquid soap holds 2.4 liters. How many liters of soap are in 4.5 bottles?

3. A small order of onion rings can have as much as 67.5 milligrams of sodium (salt). How many milligrams of sodium can be in $\frac{1}{2}$ serving?

4. One teaspoon of strawberry topping has 46.33 calories. How many calories are there in 3 teaspoons?

5. One order of french fries from a well-known fast-food restaurant contains 17.7 grams of fat. If you eat 3 orders, how much fat will you eat?

6. One serving of potato chips has 10.1 grams of fat. The whole bag of chips holds 12 servings. If you eat the whole bag, how many grams of fat have you eaten?

7. Three breadsticks have 1.5 grams of fat. How much fat do 5 breadsticks have?

Explain your estimation strategies for Questions 8–12. Then find exact answers.

8. 21.7×4.2

9. 1.2×0.54

10. 4.5×4.5

11. 0.4×6.07

12. 0.98×1.02

254   SG • Grade 5 • Unit 7 • Lesson 6   Paper-and-Pencil Decimal Multiplication

Student Guide - page 254 *(Answers on p. 124)*

At a Glance

Math Facts and Daily Practice and Problems

DPP Bit O reviews the facts. Task P provides practice estimating sums and differences with decimals.

Teaching the Activity

1. Use the *Paper-and-Pencil Decimal Multiplication* Activity Pages in the *Student Guide* to review the rule for placing decimal points in products.
2. In **Question 1** students describe the rule in their own words.
3. In **Questions 2–5** students place the decimal point in the product of a multiplication problem involving decimals. They also use estimation.

Homework

Assign the Homework section in the *Student Guide.*

Assessment

Use the *Decimal Quiz* as an assessment of students' skills.

Answer Key is on pages 124–125.

Notes:

Decimal Quiz

1. Place these decimals in order from smallest to largest:

$$1.03 \quad\quad 0.222 \quad\quad 0.4 \quad\quad 0.47$$

2. **A.** Write $\frac{426}{1000}$ as a decimal.

   B. Round the decimal in part A to the nearest hundredth.

3. Add: $4.53 + 0.672$ 4. Subtract: $4.53 - 0.672$

Estimate the answer to the following multiplication problems. Explain your estimates.

5. $3.56 \times .5$ 6. 12.67×0.9 7. 45×1.9

Use a paper-and-pencil method to solve the following problems.

8. $6.9 \times 1.5 =$ 9. $9.45 \times 0.3 =$

In Lesson 5, you solved multiplication problems with decimals. You looked for a pattern in the problems to help you place the decimal point in the answer. Lee Yah thinks of the rule this way: the sum of the number of digits after the decimal points in the factors should equal the number of digits after the decimal point in the product.

"In my problem, there is one digit after the decimal point in 3.7 and one digit after the decimal point in 1.5. That's a total of two digits after the decimal points in the factors, so there should be two digits after the decimal point in the product, 5.55," said Lee Yah.

1. A. Use your own words to tell how to place the decimal point in the answer to a multiplication problem with decimals. Use this problem as an example:

$$\begin{array}{r} 2.34 \\ \times\,0.6 \\ \hline 24 \\ 180 \\ \underline{1200} \\ 1404 \end{array}$$

B. Does your answer make sense? Estimate the answer to 2.34 × 0.6.

Use a paper-and-pencil method to solve the problems below. Use the rule or estimation to place the decimal point in the product.

2. 3.4
    × 0.4

3. .47
    × 7.9

4. .003
    × 0.8

5. 5.42
    × .5

Paper-and-Pencil Decimal Multiplication   SG • Grade 5 • Unit 7 • Lesson 6   **253**

Student Guide - page 253

Solve the following problems. Estimate to check and see if your answers are reasonable.

1. A cheeseburger from a popular fast-food restaurant has 5.7 grams of saturated fat. If you eat $2\frac{1}{2}$ cheeseburgers, how much saturated fat will you eat?

2. A bottle of liquid soap holds 2.4 liters. How many liters of soap are in 4.5 bottles?

3. A small order of onion rings can have as much as 67.5 milligrams of sodium (salt). How many milligrams of sodium can be in $\frac{1}{2}$ serving?

4. One teaspoon of strawberry topping has 46.33 calories. How many calories are there in 3 teaspoons?

5. One order of french fries from a well-known fast-food restaurant contains 17.7 grams of fat. If you eat 3 orders, how much fat will you eat?

6. One serving of potato chips has 10.1 grams of fat. The whole bag of chips holds 12 servings. If you eat the whole bag, how many grams of fat have you eaten?

7. Three breadsticks have 1.5 grams of fat. How much fat do 5 breadsticks have?

Explain your estimation strategies for Questions 8–12. Then find exact answers.

8. 21.7 × 4.2

9. 1.2 × 0.54

10. 4.5 × 4.5

11. 0.4 × 6.07

12. 0.98 × 1.02

254 SG • Grade 5 • Unit 7 • Lesson 6   Paper-and-Pencil Decimal Multiplication

Student Guide - page 254

Student Guide (p. 253)

1. A. Descriptions will vary. There are two digits after the decimal point in 2.34 and one digit after the decimal point in 0.6. So there should be three digits after the decimal point in the product, giving the answer 1.404.

 B. Estimates will vary. One possible estimate: 2 × 0.5 = 1. So 1.404 is a reasonable answer.

2. 1.36

3. 3.713

4. 0.0024*

5. 2.71

Student Guide (p. 254)

Homework

1. 14.25 grams

2. 10.8 kilograms

3. 33.75 milligrams

4. 138.99 calories

5. 53.1 grams

6. 121.2 grams

7. 7.5 grams

For Questions 8–12, estimation strategies will vary.

8. 22 × 4 = 88; 91.14

9. Half of one is one-half; 0.648

10. Round the first 4.5 down to 4 and the second 4.5 up to 5, then 4 × 5 = 20; 20.25

11. Half of six is three; 2.428

12. 1 × 1 = 1; 0.9996

---

*Answers and/or discussion are included in the Lesson Guide.

Unit Resource Guide (p. 123)

Decimal Quiz

1. $0.222 < 0.4 < 0.47 < 1.03$

2. **A.** 0.462   **B.** 0.43

3. 5.202

4. 3.858

5. 3.56 is close to 4 and .5 is $\frac{1}{2}$. Therefore, the product should be close to 2.

6. 12.67 is close to 13 and 0.9 is close to 1. Therefore, the product should be close to 13.

7. 1.9 is close to 2. Therefore the product should be close to 90.

8. 10.35

$$
\begin{array}{r}
6.9 \\
\times 1.5 \\
\hline
45 \\
300 \\
90 \\
600 \\
\hline
10.35
\end{array}
$$

9. 2.835

$$
\begin{array}{r}
9.45 \\
\times 0.3 \\
\hline
15 \\
120 \\
2700 \\
\hline
2.835
\end{array}
$$

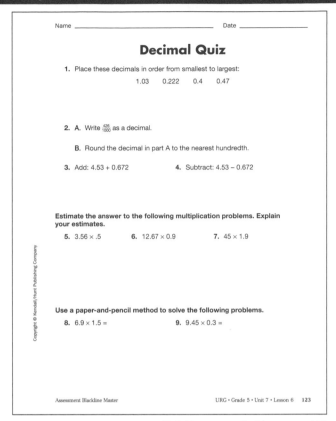

Unit Resource Guide - page 123

Lesson 7

Flipping One Coin

Lesson Overview

Estimated Class Sessions

1

Students predict the number of times heads will show if they flip a coin 40 times. They then flip a coin and compare their results with their predictions. They discuss the fact that flipping a head or a tail is equally likely (each has probability $\frac{1}{2}$). They explore other situations that have outcomes that are not equally likely.

Key Content

- Collecting and analyzing data from a random process.
- Understanding that random events are predictable "over the long run."
- Defining probability.
- Exploring situations that have outcomes that are not equally likely.

Key Vocabulary

- certain
- equally likely
- impossible
- probability

Homework

Assign Part 8 of the Home Practice in the *Discovery Assignment Book*.

Curriculum Sequence

Before This Unit

Many activities in first, second, and third grades introduce students to probability through sampling along with basic data collection and analysis. The first formal study of probability begins in fourth grade in Unit 14 *Chancy Predictions: An Introduction to Probability.* In that unit, students investigate the probabilities involved with rolling a number cube and spinning a spinner.

Materials List

Supplies and Copies

Student	Teacher
Supplies for Each Student Group • penny • small paper cup, optional • small cloth for tossing coins to muffle the sound, optional	**Supplies**
Copies • 1 copy of *Three-column Data Table* per student, optional (*Unit Resource Guide* Page 132)	**Copies/Transparencies**

All blackline masters including assessment, transparency, and DPP masters are also on the Teacher Resource CD.

Student Books

Flipping One Coin (*Student Guide* Pages 255–257)

Daily Practice and Problems and Home Practice

DPP items Q–R (*Unit Resource Guide* Page 25)
Home Practice Part 8 (*Discovery Assignment Book* Page 100)

Note: Classrooms whose pacing differs significantly from the suggested pacing of the units should use the Math Facts Calendar in Section 4 of the *Facts Resource Guide* to ensure students receive the complete math facts program.

Suggestions for using the DPPs are on page 130.

Q. Bit: Decimals (URG p. 25)

Write a decimal:

1. between 5 and 6

2. between 1 and 2

3. just a little bigger than 3

4. just a little less than 9

5. between $\frac{1}{2}$ and .9

6. between 6.5 and 7

R. Task: Adding Lengths (URG p. 25)

1. A. Draw a line segment that is 4.6 cm long. Label it $\overline{CD}$.

   B. Draw line segment $\overline{DE}$ to the right of $\overline{CD}$ that is 3.7 cm.

   C. Measure from C to E. Does $\overline{CE}$ measure 4.6 cm + 3.7 cm?

2. Model 6.2 + 4.9 by drawing two line segments $\overline{RS}$ and $\overline{ST}$.

3. Add 6.2 + 4.9. Measure your line segment ($\overline{RT}$). Does $\overline{RT}$ measure 6.2 cm + 4.9 cm?

Tell students you are going to flip a coin and ask them to predict whether it will come up heads or tails.

- *Do they think one side is more likely to show than the other?*
- *Do they understand that the side showing after the flip doesn't depend on the side that was showing before the flip (as long as the coin spins around many times in the air)?*
- *Do they realize that the probability of heads showing is $\frac{1}{2}$ or 50%?*

Flip the coin and ask whether the result agrees with their prediction. Ask whether the same side would come up each time if you were to flip the coin several times. This is what they will investigate in this activity.

Ask students to follow the instructions on the *Flipping One Coin* Activity Pages in the *Student Guide.* In **Question 1,** they predict how many times heads and how many times tails will show in 40 flips. Then, in **Questions 2–4,** they flip a coin 40 times, record their data, and compare their predictions with their results.

From what they know about probability, many students will be able to predict that heads will come up about half the time, or in about 20 out of 40 flips. However, this does not mean that heads will come up exactly half the time, as shown in the sample table in Figure 27. However, it is true that if they flip the coin many times, the fraction of heads that appears will be close to one-half *(Question 5).*

Outcome	Predicted Number of Flips	Actual Number of Flips
H	20	23
T	20	17

Figure 27: *Sample data table from flipping one coin 40 times*

TIMS Tip

Some students may prefer to shake their coins in a small paper cup. Flipping onto a soft cloth, such as a wash cloth, will reduce the noise. Students may need to practice flipping their coins before they start recording their data. It is important that the coins flip over many times while in the air or the cup.

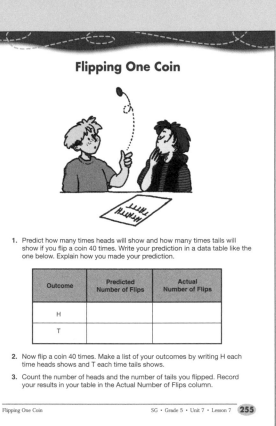

Flipping One Coin

1. Predict how many times heads will show and how many times tails will show if you flip a coin 40 times. Write your prediction in a data table like the one below. Explain how you made your prediction.

Outcome	Predicted Number of Flips	Actual Number of Flips
H		
T		

2. Now flip a coin 40 times. Make a list of your outcomes by writing H each time heads shows and T each time tails shows.

3. Count the number of heads and the number of tails you flipped. Record your results in your table in the Actual Number of Flips column.

Flipping One Coin   SG • Grade 5 • Unit 7 • Lesson 7   **255**

Student Guide - page 255 (Answers on p. 133)

4. Discuss what happened. Compare your prediction with your actual number of flips. Explain any differences.

5. What do you think will happen if you flip the coin 100 times? 1000 times?

Probability Discussions

Probability is a measure of how likely an event is to happen. Probabilities can be expressed as fractions, decimals, or percents. Events that are **certain** to happen have probability 1 or 100% (since 100% means <u>one</u> whole). Events that are **impossible** have probability 0 or 0%. All other events have probabilities between 0 and 1, or between 0% and 100%.

The closer the probability of an event is to one, or 100%, the more likely the event is to happen. When the weather forecaster reports a 95% or 0.95 probability of rain, we can be pretty sure it will rain. However, if the probability of rain is 5%, or 0.05, you probably won't need an umbrella.

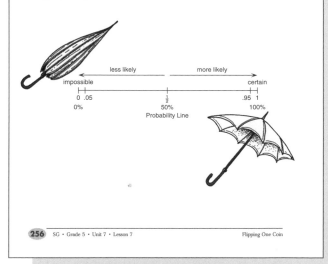

256 SG • Grade 5 • Unit 7 • Lesson 7   Flipping One Coin

Student Guide - page 256 (Answers on p. 133)

Since flipping heads is just as likely as flipping tails, we expect that heads will show about half the time when a coin is flipped many times. The probability of flipping heads is $\frac{1}{2}$.

6. Did you get heads about half the time when you flipped your coin?

With coin flipping, there are two possible outcomes—heads or tails—and each has a probability of $\frac{1}{2}$. We say that flipping heads and flipping tails are **equally likely** since the probability that each will happen is the same. However, there are other situations with two possible outcomes, which are not equally likely. Consider some of the examples below.

7. A. Right- or left-handed. How many of the students in your class are right-handed, and how many are left-handed? Based on your class's data, do you think the probability of being right-handed is more or less than one-half?

B. Right or left thumb. Clasp your hands together in front of you. Is your right thumb on top, as in the picture, or is your left thumb on top? Most people clasp their hands the same way each time they do this. Based on your class's data, do you think the probability of being a person who places the right thumb on top is more or less than $\frac{1}{2}$?

C. Boy or girl baby. Was the firstborn child in your family a girl or a boy? Based on data from the families of all the students in your class, do you think the probability of having a girl firstborn is more than, less than, or about equal to $\frac{1}{2}$?

Flipping One Coin   SG • Grade 5 • Unit 7 • Lesson 7   **257**

Student Guide - page 257 (Answers on p. 133)

Name _____ Date _____

PART 8 **The Swim Meet**
Choose an appropriate method to solve each of the following problems. For some questions you may need to find an exact answer, while for others you may only need an estimate. For each question, you may choose to use paper and pencil, mental math, or a calculator. Use a separate sheet of paper to explain how you solved each problem.

1. Shannon is on the swim team. She swam the backstroke in 7 meets. Her times for each race were 53.19 seconds, 49.67 seconds, 47.30 seconds, 43.86 seconds, 46.07 seconds, 45.87 seconds, and 45.91 seconds. What was Shannon's average speed for the backstroke during these meets? (Use the mean.)

2. A four-person team is needed to swim the medley relay. Each team member swims 50 meters using a different stroke. During one relay, Lin swam 50 meters using the butterfly stroke in 59.53 seconds, Shannon swam the backstroke in 46.12 seconds, Blanca swam the breaststroke in 53.27 seconds, and Grace finished with the freestyle stroke in 36.41 seconds.
   A. How many minutes and seconds did it take the team to complete the entire relay?
   B. What is the total distance that the relay team swam?

3. During the first swim meet of the season, Frank swam the 50-meter breaststroke event in 57.62 seconds. During the final meet of the season, he swam the 50-meter breaststroke in 44.51 seconds. How many seconds faster did Frank swim the 50-meter breaststroke at the end of the season than at the beginning?

4. During one swim meet Edward swam in 5 different events. He swam the 100-meter individual medley in 1 minute 38.30 seconds, the 50-meter butterfly in 42.48 seconds, the 50-meter breaststroke in 44.80 seconds, the 50-meter freestyle in 32.83 seconds, and the 50-meter backstroke in 45.87 seconds.
   A. How many meters did he swim during this meet?
   B. About how many minutes did Edward spend swimming during this meet?

5. The final swim meet of the season began at 8:30 A.M. It ended at 4:45 P.M. How long was the swim meet?

6. Parents held a bake sale during each meet to raise money for the team. During one meet, the parents sold cupcakes for $.25 each. They sold 42 cupcakes. How much money did they get for the cupcakes?

7. The ribbons for the winners cost $.08 each. During the swim season the team used 648 ribbons. About how much did the team spend on the ribbons for this season?

100 DAB • Grade 5 • Unit 7   DECIMALS AND PROBABILITY

Discovery Assignment Book - page 100 (Answers on p. 134)

Ask students to read the Probability Discussions section. It defines a **probability** as a number that describes how likely an event is to happen. A probability is a number from 0 to 1, or equivalently, a percent from 0% to 100%. Events that are **impossible** have probability 0. The more likely an event is to happen, the larger the probability. Events that are **certain** have the largest probability: 1 or 100%.

In *Question 6,* students decide that the probability of flipping a head is $\frac{1}{2}$ or 50%. Ask students to think of other events and to estimate the probability the events will occur.

• *What is the probability students will have homework tonight?*

• *What is the probability it will snow where they live this winter?*

We say that flipping heads and flipping tails are **equally likely** to occur since the probability that each will happen is the same. *Questions 7A–7C* describe other situations with two possible outcomes: being right- or left-handed, placing right or left thumb on top when clasping hands together, having a firstborn girl or firstborn boy. Discuss these situations with your class and help them to decide which pairs of events are equally likely. Your discussion will depend on your class's results, but your data will probably suggest that *Questions 7A–7B* describe events that are not equally likely. The events in *Question 7C,* having a girl or a boy firstborn child are almost equally likely. However, as with coin flipping, you should not be surprised if you do not get exactly half firstborn boys and half firstborn girls in your sample.

> ## Content Note
> Actually, the probability of having a boy is slightly greater than the probability of having a girl, but we will assume for discussion that boys and girls are equally likely.

Homework and Practice

• Assign DPP items Q and R. Item Q involves number sense with decimals. Task R includes measurement with decimals.

• Assign Home Practice Part 8 for practice with word problems involving decimals.

Answers for Part 8 of the Home Practice are in the Answer Key at the end of this lesson and at the end of this unit.

At a Glance

Math Facts and Daily Practice and Problems

DPP items Q and R both involve work with decimals.

Teaching the Activity

1. Ask students to predict whether a coin you will flip will come up heads or tails. Probe their understanding of probability.
2. Flip a coin. Ask whether the same side will come up each time.
3. Using the questions in the *Student Guide,* students predict the number of times heads will show and the number of times tails will show in 40 flips. *(Question 1)*
4. Students flip coins 40 times and record data in a hand-drawn data table. *(Questions 2–3)*
5. Discuss the results. *(Questions 4–6)*
6. Discuss that probability is a number from 0 to 1. Probabilities can be expressed as fractions, decimals, or percents. Students describe events and estimate their probabilities.
7. Discuss *Questions 7A–7C.* Which of the events are equally likely?

Homework

Assign Part 8 of the Home Practice in the *Discovery Assignment Book.*

Answer Key is on pages 133–134.

Notes:

Name _____ Date _____

_____

Three-column Data Table, Blackline Master

Student Guide (pp. 255–257)

1.–7. Answers will vary. See the Lesson Guide for sample data (Figure 27) and discussion of the questions.*

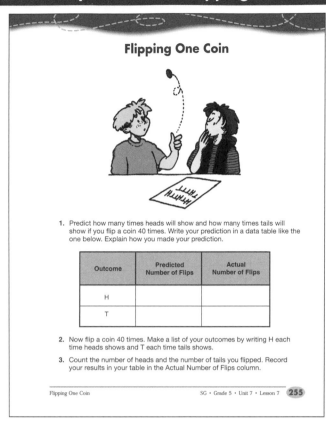

Flipping One Coin

1. Predict how many times heads will show and how many times tails will show if you flip a coin 40 times. Write your prediction in a data table like the one below. Explain how you made your prediction.

Outcome	Predicted Number of Flips	Actual Number of Flips
H		
T		

2. Now flip a coin 40 times. Make a list of your outcomes by writing H each time heads shows and T each time tails shows.

3. Count the number of heads and the number of tails you flipped. Record your results in your table in the Actual Number of Flips column.

Flipping One Coin   SG • Grade 5 • Unit 7 • Lesson 7   **255**

Student Guide - page 255

---

4. Discuss what happened. Compare your prediction with your actual number of flips. Explain any differences.

5. What do you think will happen if you flip the coin 100 times? 1000 times?

Probability Discussions

Probability is a measure of how likely an event is to happen. Probabilities can be expressed as fractions, decimals, or percents. Events that are **certain** to happen have probability 1 or 100% (since 100% means <u>one</u> whole). Events that are **impossible** have probability 0 or 0%. All other events have probabilities between 0 and 1, or between 0% and 100%.

The closer the probability of an event is to one, or 100%, the more likely the event is to happen. When the weather forecaster reports a 95% or 0.95 probability of rain, we can be pretty sure it will rain. However, if the probability of rain is 5%, or 0.05, you probably won't need an umbrella.

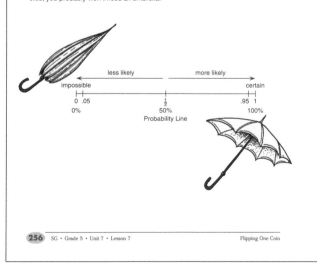

256 SG • Grade 5 • Unit 7 • Lesson 7   Flipping One Coin

Student Guide - page 256

Since flipping heads is just as likely as flipping tails, we expect that heads will show about half the time when a coin is flipped many times. The probability of flipping heads is $\frac{1}{2}$.

6. Did you get heads about half the time when you flipped your coin?

With coin flipping, there are two possible outcomes—heads or tails—and each has a probability of $\frac{1}{2}$. We say that flipping heads and flipping tails are **equally likely** since the probability that each will happen is the same. However, there are other situations with two possible outcomes, which are not equally likely. Consider some of the examples below.

7. **A.** <u>Right- or left-handed.</u> How many of the students in your class are right-handed, and how many are left-handed? Based on your class's data, do you think the probability of being right-handed is more or less than one-half?

B. <u>Right or left thumb.</u> Clasp your hands together in front of you. Is your right thumb on top, as in the picture, or is your left thumb on top? Most people clasp their hands the same way each time they do this. Based on your class's data, do you think the probability of being a person who places the right thumb on top is more or less than $\frac{1}{2}$?

C. <u>Boy or girl baby.</u> Was the firstborn child in your family a girl or a boy? Based on data from the families of all the students in your class, do you think the probability of having a girl firstborn is more than, less than, or about equal to $\frac{1}{2}$?

Flipping One Coin   SG • Grade 5 • Unit 7 • Lesson 7   **257**

Student Guide - page 257

*Answers and/or discussion are included in the Lesson Guide.

Name _____ Date _____

PART 8 The Swim Meet

Choose an appropriate method to solve each of the following problems. For
some questions you may need to find an exact answer, while for others you
may only need an estimate. For each question, you may choose to use paper
and pencil, mental math, or a calculator. Use a separate sheet of paper to
explain how you solved each problem.

1. Shannon is on the swim team. She swam the backstroke in 7 meets. Her
times for each race were 53.19 seconds, 49.67 seconds, 47.30 seconds,
43.86 seconds, 46.07 seconds, 45.87 seconds, and 45.91 seconds.
What was Shannon's average speed for the backstroke during these meets?
(Use the mean.)

2. A four-person team is needed to swim the medley relay. Each team member
swims 50 meters using a different stroke. During one relay, Lin swam
50 meters using the butterfly stroke in 59.53 seconds, Shannon swam
the backstroke in 46.12 seconds, Blanca swam the breaststroke in
53.27 seconds, and Grace finished with the freestyle stroke in 36.41 seconds.

   A. How many minutes and seconds did it take the team to complete the
   entire relay?

   B. What is the total distance that the relay team swam?

3. During the first swim meet of the season, Frank swam the 50-meter
breaststroke event in 57.62 seconds. During the final meet of the season, he
swam the 50-meter breaststroke in 44.51 seconds. How many seconds
faster did Frank swim the 50-meter breaststroke at the end of the season
than at the beginning?

4. During one swim meet Edward swam in 5 different events. He swam the
100-meter individual medley in 1 minute 38.30 seconds, the 50-meter
butterfly in 42.48 seconds, the 50-meter breaststroke in 44.80 seconds, the
50-meter freestyle in 32.83 seconds, and the 50-meter backstroke in
45.87 seconds.

   A. How many meters did he swim during this meet?

   B. About how many minutes did Edward spend swimming during this meet?

5. The final swim meet of the season began at 8:30 A.M. It ended at 4:45 P.M.
How long was the swim meet?

6. Parents held a bake sale during each meet to raise money for the team.
During one meet, the parents sold cupcakes for $.25 each. They sold
42 cupcakes. How much money did they get for the cupcakes?

7. The ribbons for the winners cost $.08 each. During the swim season the
team used 648 ribbons. About how much did the team spend on the ribbons
for this season?

Copyright © Kendall/Hunt Publishing Company

100 DAB • Grade 5 • Unit 7   DECIMALS AND PROBABILITY

Discovery Assignment Book - page 100

Discovery Assignment Book (p. 100)

Home Practice*

Part 8. The Swim Meet

1. 47.41 seconds

2. **A.** 3 minutes and 15.33 seconds

   B. 200 meters

3. 13.11 seconds

4. **A.** 300 meters

   B. Answers will vary. One possible estimate
   is $1\frac{1}{2}$ min $+ \frac{1}{2}$ min $+ \frac{1}{2}$ min $+ \frac{1}{2}$ min $+ 1$ min
   or about 4 min.

5. 8 hours and 15 minutes

6. $10.50

7. Estimates will vary. One possible estimate is:
   $600 \times 10¢ = 6000¢$ or $60.00.

*Answers for all the Home Practice in the *Discovery Assignment Book* are at the end of the unit.

134   URG • Grade 5 • Unit 7 • Lesson 7 • Answer Key

Lesson 8

Flipping Two Coins

Lesson Overview

Estimated Class Sessions

3

Students investigate probability by gathering data: a penny and a nickel are flipped repeatedly and the number of heads showing is recorded. The percentages of trials showing 0, 1, and 2 heads are calculated and graphed, then compared with the respective probabilities. Data is compared for 10, 100, and 1000 trials (after pooling data with classmates). This comparison helps students understand that probability predicts the behavior of random systems over the long run.

Key Content

- Analyzing fair and unfair games.
- Computing probabilities for all possible outcomes when two coins are flipped.
- Expressing probabilities as fractions, decimals, and percents.
- Collecting, organizing, graphing, and analyzing data.
- Making and interpreting bar graphs.
- Using probabilities to predict.
- Comparing probabilities with real-world data.

Key Vocabulary

- fair game
- probability

Math Facts

DPP items S and W review the multiplication and division facts.

Homework

1. *Questions 1–4* provide practice translating fractions, decimals, and percents. Assign these questions before students analyze their data.
2. Assign *Question 5* after students complete the lab. They play a game and use what they learned from the lab to decide if it is fair or unfair.
3. Assign Part 7 of the Home Practice.

Assessment

1. Assign points to one or more sections of the lab and grade them as an assessment.
2. As students analyze their group data, record their abilities to make and interpret bar graphs on the *Observational Assessment Record.*
3. Transfer appropriate documentation to students' *Individual Assessment Record Sheets.*

Materials List

Supplies and Copies

Student	Teacher
Supplies for Each Student Group • calculators • penny • nickel • small paper cup, optional • small cloth for tossing coins onto to muffle the sound, optional	**Supplies**
Copies • 3 copies of *Centimeter Graph Paper* per student (*Unit Resource Guide* Page 147)	**Copies/Transparencies** • 1 transparency of *Coin Flipping Data Tables,* optional (*Discovery Assignment Book* Page 121) • 1 copy of *Observational Assessment Record* to be used throughout this unit (*Unit Resource Guide* Pages 13–14)

All blackline masters including assessment, transparency, and DPP masters are also on the Teacher Resource CD.

Student Books
Flipping Two Coins (*Student Guide* Pages 258–264)
100 Two-Coin Flips (*Discovery Assignment Book* Page 119)
Coin Flipping Data Tables (*Discovery Assignment Book* Page 121)
Comparing Probability with Results (*Discovery Assignment Book* Page 123)

Daily Practice and Problems and Home Practice
DPP items S–X (*Unit Resource Guide* Pages 26–28)
Home Practice Part 7 (*Discovery Assignment Book* Page 99)

Note: Classrooms whose pacing differs significantly from the suggested pacing of the units should use the Math Facts Calendar in Section 4 of the *Facts Resource Guide* to ensure students receive the complete math facts program.

Assessment Tools
Observational Assessment Record (*Unit Resource Guide* Pages 13–14)
Individual Assessment Record Sheet (*Teacher Implementation Guide,* Assessment section)

Daily Practice and Problems

Suggestions for using the DPPs are on page 144.

S. Bit: Reviewing the Facts (URG p. 26)

Solve the given fact. Then name the other related fact or facts in the same fact family.

A. $6 \div 3 =$ 　　　　B. $8 \times 8 =$

C. $35 \div 7 =$ 　　　D. $20 \div 5 =$

E. $9 \times 6 =$ 　　　F. $27 \div 9 =$

T. Task: Practice (URG p. 26)

Solve the following using paper and pencil. Estimate to be sure your answers are reasonable.

A. $34 + 78 =$ 　　　B. $582 - 465 =$

C. $2708 \times 6 =$ 　　D. $89 \times 12 =$

E. $2649 \div 6 =$ 　　F. $5893 + 3075 =$

U. Bit: Missing Decimal Points (URG p. 27)

Professor Peabody forgot to put decimal points in the numbers below. He does know that the "6" in each number stands for six-tenths.

Put a decimal point in each number so the 6 stands for six-tenths. Now say the numbers aloud to a partner.

A. 1360 　　B. 1206 　　C. 603

D. 126 　　E. 367 　　F. 1634

V. Task: Multiplying Decimals
(URG p. 27)

Estimate the products. Then solve each problem using paper and pencil.

A. $3.4 \times 2.1 =$ 　　B. $5.6 \times 10.4 =$

C. $8.2 \times 8.9 =$ 　　D. $0.89 \times .95 =$

E. $18 \times .96 =$ 　　F. $28.85 \times 4 =$

W. Bit: Reviewing the Facts (URG p. 27)

Solve the given fact. Then name the other related fact or facts in the same fact family.

A. $7 \times 3 =$ 　　　B. $36 \div 6 =$

C. $72 \div 8 =$ 　　　D. $4 \times 9 =$

E. $50 \div 5 =$ 　　　F. $7 \times 7 =$

X. Challenge: Rich in Pounds
(URG p. 28)

Four quarters (25¢) weigh 0.05 pound. You need 7200 quarters to equal the average weight of a 12-year-old.

1. What is the average weight of a 12-year-old?

2. How much do 7200 quarters equal in dollars and cents?

Flipping Two Coins

Game: How Many Heads?

Players

This is a game for 3 players.
One person is the 0-Heads Player,
the second is the 1-Head Player,
and the third is the 2-Heads Player.

Materials

- 2 coins
- How Many Heads? table

Rules

Flip 2 coins.
If 0 heads show, then the 0-Heads Player gets a point.
If 1 head shows, then the 1-Head Player gets a point.
If 2 heads show, then the 2-Heads Player gets a point.

The first player to score 10 points wins.

1. Play several games. For each game, keep score in a table like this.

How Many Heads?

Player	Points	
	Tallies	Total
0-Heads Player		
1-Head Player		
2-Heads Player		

Student Guide - page 258 (Answers on p. 148)

---

2. If you could play again, which player would you choose to be and why?

3. Mathematicians say that a game is **fair** if all players have an equal chance of winning. Tell whether this is a mathematically fair game and why.

Lab: Flipping Two Coins

In this lab, you will flip two coins, a penny and a nickel, 100 times. For each trial, or time you flip two coins, you will count how many heads show.

4. Before the lab, predict how many times each number of heads will show in your 100 trials. Make a table like this to record your prediction. Explain how you made your prediction.

Prediction Data Table

Number of Heads	Predicted Number of Trials
0	
1	
2	

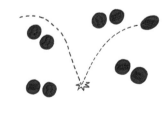

Student Guide - page 259 (Answers on p. 148)

Before the Lab

Ask students to play the game *How Many Heads?* in the *Flipping Two Coins* Activity Pages in the *Student Guide* as an introduction to the lab. This is a game for three players. The players flip two coins (they can use a penny and a nickel) and count the number of heads that show. One player is designated the 0-Heads Player, who will receive one point if zero heads show. The next player is the 1-Head Player who will receive a point if one head shows, and the third player is the 2-Heads Player who will receive a point if two heads show.

Students will notice after playing the game a few times that one head shows more often (about twice as often) than either zero heads or two heads. The reason for this will be more apparent after the lab. The 1-Head Player has a better chance of winning, and, for this reason, the game is inherently unfair. A **fair game** gives players an equal chance of winning. Students sometimes confuse "playing fair" (taking turns, not cheating, etc.) with the mathematical concept of a fair game. Explain that mathematicians categorize games as **fair** or **unfair** based on the probabilities the players have of winning, rather than on sportsmanship.

You can assign **Questions 1–4** in the Homework section of the *Flipping Two Coins* Activity Pages in the *Student Guide* at this time. These questions practice skills students need to complete the lab.

Question 5 in the Homework section of the *Student Guide* includes an example of a fair game. After the lab, students can apply what they learned to help them decide whether this game is fair or unfair and to explain their reasons.

Teaching the Lab

Students flip two coins, a penny and a nickel, 100 times. Then they combine their data with the other groups' data to get the results of 1000 flips.

Question 4 in the Lab: Flipping Two Coins section asks students to predict the number of times 0, 1, and 2 heads will come up in their 100 trials. Encourage students to base their predictions on their experience with the game. In the game, 1 head showing is twice as likely as 0 heads showing or 2 heads showing. So, if the two coins are flipped 100 times, a sophisticated prediction is fifty 1-head flips, twenty-five 0-head flips, and twenty-five 2-head flips. Encourage students to explain their predictions.

Part 1 Data Tables

After students make their predictions, they are ready to collect their data *(Question 5)*. They will record the outcome of the penny first and the nickel second. For example, if the penny shows tails and the nickel shows heads, they will record TH. (They could use two pennies instead of a penny and a nickel and get similar results, but it may help them to see that there are two ways to get 1 head (HT and TH) if they use two easily distinguishable coins). Each flip will result in one of these four outcomes: HH, HT, TH, TT.

Students record their outcomes on the *100 Two-Coin Flips* Activity Page in the *Discovery Assignment Book.* Sample data are shown in Figure 28. Next, they summarize the results of their first 10 flips *(Question 6)* and their 100 flips *(Question 7)* using the first two tables on the *Coin Flipping Data Tables* Activity Page in the *Discovery Assignment Book,* as shown in Figures 29 and 30.

100 Two-Coin Flips

Trial	Outcome	Number of Heads	Trial	Outcome	Number of Heads	Trial	Outcome	Number of Heads	Trial	Outcome	Number of Heads
1.	HH	2	26.	HT	1	51.	TT	0	76.	TT	0
2.	HT	1	27.	HT	1	52.	TH	1	77.	TH	1
3.	HH	2	28.	TH	1	53.	HT	1	78.	HH	2
4.	TT	0	29.	HT	1	54.	HT	1	79.	TH	1
5.	HH	2	30.	HT	1	55.	HH	2	80.	HT	1
6.	TT	0	31.	TH	1	56.	TH	1	81.	HH	2
7.	TT	0	32.	TH	1	57.	HT	1	82.	HT	1
8.	TH	1	33.	HH	2	58.	TT	0	83.	HH	2
9.	TH	1	34.	HH	2	59.	HH	2	84.	HT	1
10.	TH	1	35.	TH	1	60.	TH	1	85.	TH	1
11.	HT	1	36.	HH	2	61.	TT	0	86.	TH	1
12.	TH	1	37.	TH	1	62.	HH	2	87.	HT	1
13.	TH	1	38.	HH	2	63.	HH	2	88.	HH	2
14.	TT	0	39.	TH	1	64.	HT	1	89.	TH	1
15.	TH	1	40.	HH	2	65.	HT	1	90.	TH	1
16.	HH	2	41.	HH	2	66.	TH	1	91.	HH	2
17.	TT	0	42.	TT	0	67.	HT	1	92.	TT	0
18.	HT	1	43.	HT	1	68.	HH	2	93.	HT	1
19.	TH	1	44.	HT	1	69.	HH	2	94.	HT	1
20.	TH	1	45.	HH	2	70.	TH	1	95.	TT	0
21.	HH	2	46.	TT	0	71.	HH	2	96.	TT	0
22.	HT	1	47.	TH	1	72.	TT	0	97.	TT	0
23.	TH	1	48.	HH	2	73.	HT	1	98.	HH	2
24.	TT	0	49.	HH	2	74.	TH	1	99.	TT	0
25.	HH	2	50.	HT	1	75.	TT	0	100.	HH	1

Figure 28: *Sample data from flipping two coins*

Content Note

Although the first phase of most labs in the TIMS Laboratory Method includes drawing a picture, this investigation begins with the game *How Many Heads?* Probability questions that students will investigate in the lab are introduced as students play the game and analyze the results.

TIMS Tip

Divide the class into 10 groups for flipping, so the total number of flips is 1000. If you have fewer than ten groups in your class, have volunteers carry out the additional sets of 100 flips.

Data Tables

5. Now flip the penny and the nickel 100 times. Record your trials in the table on the *100 Two-Coin Flips* Activity Page in the *Discovery Assignment Book.* Write the outcome of the penny first and the nickel second. For example, if the penny shows heads and the nickel shows tails, then record HT in the outcome column.

100 Two-Coin Flips

Trial	Outcome	Number of Heads
1.	HT	1
2.	HH	2
3.	TH	1
4.	TT	0
5.	TH	1

6. Look at the data for your first 10 trials only. Complete the 10-Trial Table on the *Coin Flipping Data Tables* Activity Page in the *Discovery Assignment Book* to show the number, fraction, and percent of the first 10 trials that have 0, 1, and 2 heads. The first row shows an example. Write your data in your table.

10-Trial Table

Number of Heads	N Number of Trials Out of 10	$\frac{N}{10}$ Fraction of Trials Out of 10	Equivalent Fraction with Denominator of 100	Percent of 10 Trials
0	3	$\frac{3}{10}$	$\frac{30}{100}$	30%
1				
2				

7. Look at the data from all 100 trials. Complete the 100-Trial Table on the *Coin Flipping Data Tables* Activity Page. Show the number, fraction, and percent of your 100 trials that have 0, 1, and 2 heads.

Student Guide - page 260 (Answers on p. 149)

Name _____ Date _____

100 Two-Coin Flips

Trial	Outcome	Number of Heads	Trial	Outcome	Number of Heads	Trial	Outcome	Number of Heads	Trial	Outcome	Number of Heads
1.			26.			51.			76.		
2.			27.			52.			77.		
3.			28.			53.			78.		
4.			29.			54.			79.		
5.			30.			55.			80.		
6.			31.			56.			81.		
7.			32.			57.			82.		
8.			33.			58.			83.		
9.			34.			59.			84.		
10.			35.			60.			85.		
11.			36.			61.			86.		
12.			37.			62.			87.		
13.			38.			63.			88.		
14.			39.			64.			89.		
15.			40.			65.			90.		
16.			41.			66.			91.		
17.			42.			67.			92.		
18.			43.			68.			93.		
19.			44.			69.			94.		
20.			45.			70.			95.		
21.			46.			71.			96.		
22.			47.			72.			97.		
23.			48.			73.			98.		
24.			49.			74.			99.		
25.			50.			75.			100.		

Flipping Two Coins   DAB • Grade 5 • Unit 7 • Lesson 8 **119**

Discovery Assignment Book - page 119 *(Answers on p. 152)*

Name _____ Date _____

Coin Flipping Data Tables

10-Trial Table

Number of Heads	N Number of Trials Out of 10	N/10 Fraction of Trials Out of 10	Equivalent Fraction with Denominator of 100	Percent of 10 Trials
0				
1				
2				

100-Trial Table

Number of Heads	Number of Trials Out of 100	Fraction of Trials Out of 100	Percent of 100 Trials
0			
1			
2			

1000-Trial Table

Number of Heads	Number of Trials for Each Group										Total Number of Trials Out of 1000	Fraction of Trials Out of 1000	Decimal	Nearest Hundredth	Nearest Percent
	Gr.1	Gr.2	Gr.3	Gr.4	Gr.5	Gr.6	Gr.7	Gr.8	Gr.9	Gr.10					
0															
1															
2															

Flipping Two Coins   DAB • Grade 5 • Unit 7 • Lesson 8 **121**

Discovery Assignment Book - page 121 *(Answers on p. 152)*

10-Trial Table

Number of Heads	N Number of Trials Out of 10	$\frac{N}{10}$ Fraction of Trials Out of 10	Equivalent Fraction With Denominator of 100	Percent of 10 Trials
0	3	$\frac{3}{10}$	$\frac{30}{100}$	30%
1	4	$\frac{4}{10}$	$\frac{40}{100}$	40%
2	3	$\frac{3}{10}$	$\frac{30}{100}$	30%

Figure 29: *Data from the first 10 trials*

100-Trial Table

Number of Heads	Number of Trials Out of 100	Fraction of Trials Out of 100	Percent of 100 Trials
0	19	$\frac{19}{100}$	19%
1	52	$\frac{52}{100}$	52%
2	29	$\frac{29}{100}$	29%

Figure 30: *Data from all 100 trials*

TIMS Tip

Carefully check the percentages students enter in their tables. A common mistake occurs with fractions that do not have 100 in the denominator. For example $\frac{3}{10}$ is sometimes incorrectly written as 3% instead of 30% and $\frac{244}{1000}$ is incorrectly written as 244% instead of approximately 24%.

1000-Trial Table

Number of Heads	Number of Trials for Each Group										Total Number of Trials Out of 1000	Fraction of Trials Out of 1000	Decimal	Nearest Hundredth	Nearest Percent
	Gr.1	Gr.2	Gr.3	Gr.4	Gr.5	Gr.6	Gr.7	Gr.8	Gr.9	Gr.10					
0	19	24	22	28	19	24	33	24	26	25	244	$\frac{244}{1000}$	0.244	0.24	24%
1	52	54	54	53	51	50	41	54	43	45	497	$\frac{497}{1000}$	0.497	0.50	50%
2	29	22	24	19	30	26	26	22	31	30	259	$\frac{259}{1000}$	0.259	0.26	26%

Figure 31: *Data from 10 groups pooled to give 1000 trials*

Finally, students pool their data with the other groups to obtain results for 1000 flips and record their pooled data in the 1000-Trial Table on the *Coin Flipping Data Tables* Activity Page, as shown in Figure 31 *(Question 8).*

Part 2 Graphs

Graphs of sample data are shown in Figures 32, 33, and 34. *Question 9* asks students to make 3 graphs and to think about whether bar graphs or point graphs make more sense here. The line on a point graph suggests we can consider in-between values. For example, the line would let us predict how many times 1.5 heads show, but it doesn't make sense to talk about $1\frac{1}{2}$ heads. Since the only numbers on the horizontal axis that are meaningful are 0, 1, and 2 heads, it makes more sense to use a bar graph.

Be sure students label the axes and put the numbers on the lines, not in the spaces. Students should use the same scale on all three graphs so they will be able to compare the graphs. You may want to use a transparency of *Centimeter Graph Paper* to model the graph for the first 10 flips.

Question 10 asks students to analyze their graphs. Students should notice that the tallest bar for every graph is the middle bar—the bar for 1 head. On the graph for 1000 trials, this bar is about twice as tall as the other two bars.

8. Now collect data from 10 groups to get a total of 1000 trials. Complete the 1000-Trial Table on the *Coin Flipping Data Tables* Activity Page. Show the number, fraction, and percent of 1000 trials that have 0, 1, and 2 heads.

Graph

9. Make 3 graphs—one for each of your data tables in Questions 6, 7, and 8.
   - Plot the Number of Heads on the horizontal axis and the Percent of Trials on the vertical axis.
   - Think about whether bar graphs or point graphs make more sense here.

10. Describe your graphs.
    A. How are they alike? How are they different?
    B. Which bar is the tallest?
    C. In the 1000-Trial Graph, how many times taller is the tallest bar than the other two bars?

Explore

11. A. What are the possible outcomes when you flip 2 coins? List them.
    B. How many ways can 0 heads come up? List the way(s).
    C. How many ways can 1 head come up? List the way(s).
    D. How many ways can 2 heads come up? List the way(s).

12. How does knowing the number of ways the coins can land help you to understand why the experiment (and your graphs) turned out the way they did?

Probability

The **probability** of 2 heads (HH) when two coins are flipped is the number of ways 2 heads can show, divided by the total number of ways the coins can land.

Probability of 2 heads showing = $1 \div 4 = \frac{1}{4}$

The probability tells us about how often we can expect an event to occur when an experiment is repeated many times.

Flipping Two Coins — SG • Grade 5 • Unit 7 • Lesson 8 — **261**

Student Guide - page 261 (Answers on p. 149)

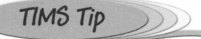

TIMS Tip

To help pool data, make a big table on the board or overhead for each group to record its 100-flip data. Then, the other groups can copy from the board rather than going to each group.

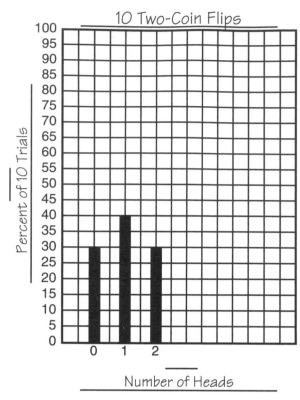

Figure 32: *Graph of the first 10 two-coin flips*

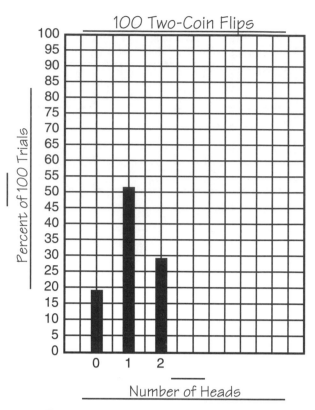

Figure 33: *Graph of 100 two-coin flips*

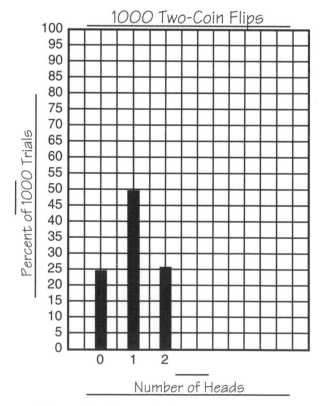

Figure 34: *Graph of 1000 two-coin flips*

Part 3 Explore

Students see in **Question 11** that there are two ways one head can come up (HT and TH), but only one way two heads can show (HH), and one way two tails can show (TT). This helps them understand why one head shows about twice as often as zero and two heads, and therefore why the bar for 1 head is twice as tall as the other bars **(Question 12).**

Content Note

Probability. The **probability** of an event occurring is equal to the number of favorable outcomes divided by the total number of possible outcomes.

Probability of an event = number of favorable outcomes/number of possible outcomes

For example, the probability of flipping two heads when flipping two coins is $\frac{1}{4}$.

$\frac{1}{4} = \frac{\text{number of favorable outcomes (HH)}}{\text{number of possible outcomes (HH, HT, TH, TT)}}$

The probability of flipping one head is $\frac{2}{4}$ or $\frac{1}{2}$.

$\frac{2}{4} = \frac{\text{number of favorable outcomes (HT, TH)}}{\text{number of possible outcomes (HH, HT, TH, TT)}}$

Another example: If one letter of the alphabet is chosen at random, the probability of choosing a vowel is $\frac{5}{26}$.

$\frac{5}{26} = \frac{\text{number of favorable outcomes (a, e, i, o, u)}}{\text{number of possible outcomes (26 total letters)}}$

Part 4 Probability

Question 14 asks students to calculate the probabilities for 0, 1, and 2 heads and to enter them in the Probabilities of Coin Flipping table on the *Comparing Probability with Results* Activity Page in the *Discovery Assignment Book.* See Figure 35. They then record the data for 10, 100, and 1000 trials in the Results of Coin Flipping table on the same page. They obtain this data from the last column of their 10-Trial, 100-Trial, and 1000-Trial Tables **(Question 15).**

Notice in the Figure 36 data that with more flips, the percents are closer to the probabilities. Remind students that probability is a way of predicting what will happen over the long run. The probability of showing one head is one-half. With many trials, this means we can expect about half will show one head, although this may not be the case in only a few trials **(Questions 13 and 16).**

13. Since the probability of 2 heads is one-fourth, we can expect 2 heads to show about one-fourth of the time, when we flip the coin many times. Did that happen in your experiment?

14. Use your answers to Question 11 to compute the probabilities of getting 0 heads and 1 head. Enter the probabilities in a probability table like the one below. Your copy is on the *Comparing Probability with Results* Activity Page in the *Discovery Assignment Book.*

Probabilities of Coin Flipping

Number of Heads	Ways Heads Can Come Up	Probability (as a fraction)	Probability (as a percent)
0			
1			
2	HH	$\frac{1}{4}$	25%

15. Use the Results of Coin Flipping table from the *Comparing Probability with Results* Activity Page. Enter the percents of the trials in your experiment that had 0, 1, and 2 heads. (Use the data from the last column of the tables in Questions 6, 7, and 8.)

Results of Coin Flipping

Number of Heads	Percent of 10 Trials	Percent of 100 Trials	Percent of 1000 Trials
0			
1			
2			

16. Compare your tables from Questions 14 and 15. What pattern do you see? Explain what is happening as more trials are made.

17. Do the results of your experiment match your predictions in Question 4? Why or why not?

262   SG • Grade 5 • Unit 7 • Lesson 8   Flipping Two Coins

Student Guide - page 262 (Answers on p. 150)

Name _____ Date _____

Comparing Probability with Results

Probabilities of Coin Flipping

Number of Heads	Ways Heads Can Come Up	Probability (as a fraction)	Probability (as a percent)
0			
1			
2			

Results of Coin Flipping

Number of Heads	Percent of 10 Trials	Percent of 100 Trials	Percent of 1000 Trials
0			
1			
2			

Flipping Two Coins   DAB • Grade 5 • Unit 7 • Lesson 8 **123**

Discovery Assignment Book - page 123 (Answers on p. 153)

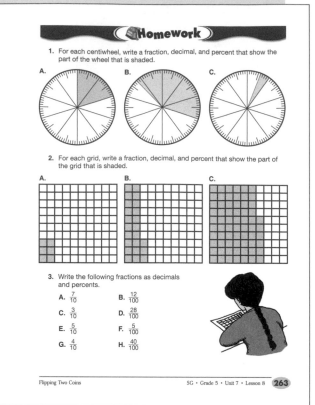

Student Guide - page 263 (Answers on p. 150)

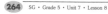

Probabilities of Coin Flipping

Number of Heads	Ways Heads Can Come Up	Probability (as a fraction)	Probability (as a percent)
0	TT	$\frac{1}{4}$	25%
1	HT or TH	$\frac{2}{4}$	50%
2	HH	$\frac{1}{4}$	25%

Figure 35: *Probabilities of 0, 1, and 2 heads*

Results of Coin Flipping

Number of Heads	Percent of 10 Trials	Percent of 100 Trials	Percent of 1000 Trials
0	30%	19%	24%
1	40%	52%	50%
2	30%	29%	26%

Figure 36: *Results of coin flipping*

Math Facts

DPP items S and W review the multiplication and division facts.

Homework and Practice

- Homework *Questions 1–4* provide practice with writing fractions, decimals, and percents. Assign them before students complete *Question 6* in the lab.

- Assign *Question 5* in the Homework section after students complete the lab. In this question, students determine whether another game, *Matching 2 Pennies,* is fair or unfair. Discuss why this game is fair, but the game *How Many Heads?* was not. Both games involve flipping two coins, with possible outcomes (HH, HT, TH, TT). In *Matching 2 Pennies,* Player 1 has two ways to get a point (HH and TT) and Player 2 also has two ways to get a point (HT and TH). They both have an equal chance of winning, so the game is fair. However, in *How Many Heads?* Player 0 and Player 2 have only one way to get a point (TT and HH, respectively), while Player 1 has two ways (HT and TH). All three players do not have an equal chance of winning, so the game is not fair.

Student Guide - page 264 (Answers on p. 151)

- Assign DPP items T, U, V, and X for practice with problem solving, operations, and decimals.
- Assign Part 7 of the Home Practice that involves probability.

Answers for Part 7 of the Home Practice are in the Answer Key at the end of this lesson and at the end of this unit.

Assessment

- To grade the lab, assign points to one or more sections. For example, if you grade the data tables students completed in *Questions 6–8* (on the *Coin Flipping Data Tables* Activity Page in the *Discovery Assignment Book),* you can assess their abilities to use fractions, decimals, and percents in the context of a lab. See the Evaluating Labs section of the Assessment section of the *Teacher Implementation Guide* for suggestions for grading all sections.
- As students analyze their group data, use the *Observational Assessment Record* and students' *Individual Assessment Record Sheet* to record students' abilities to make and interpret bar graphs.

Name _____ Date _____

PART 6 Working with Decimals
Solve the following problems using paper and pencil. Estimate to be sure your answers are reasonable.

A. 45.6 + 12.35 =   B. 0.76 + 0.043 =   C. 0.89 × 4 =

D. 7.3 − 0.53 =   E. 4.8 × 8.3 =   F. 0.67 × 2 =

G. 176.4 + 0.385 =   H. 456.07 − 128.43 =   I. 4.577 × 0.5 =

PART 7 What's the Chance?
Manny works at the miniature golf range. The owner bought 20 new balls. He bought 5 red balls, 2 white balls, 3 green balls, 7 orange balls, and 3 yellow balls. Manny put all the new balls in a bucket. In between customers, he tries a probability experiment. If Manny picks one ball, the probability that he will pick a yellow ball is $\frac{3}{20}$.

1. Without looking, he picks one ball from the bucket. Write each of the following probabilities as a fraction, decimal, and percent:
   A. The probability that he will pick a red ball.
   B. The probability that he will pick a white ball.
   C. The probability that he will pick a green ball.
   D. The probability that he will pick an orange ball.

2. What color ball will Manny most likely pick? Justify your answer.

3. Manny predicts that he will choose a red ball or an orange ball. Is this a good prediction? Why or why not?

DECIMALS AND PROBABILITY   DAB · Grade 5 · Unit 7   **99**

Discovery Assignment Book* - page 99 *(Answers on p. 151)

At a Glance

Math Facts and Daily Practice and Problems

DPP items S and W review the facts. Items T, U, V, and X provide practice.

Before the Lab

Students play *How Many Heads?* following the directions on the *Flipping Two Coins* Activity Pages in the *Student Guide. (Questions 1–3)* They discuss whether it is a fair game.

Part 1. Data Tables

1. Divide the class into 10 groups for flipping. Students predict the number of times 0, 1, and 2 heads will come up in 100 two-coin flips. Then they flip coins and record their data on the *100 Two-Coin Flips* Activity Page in the *Discovery Assignment Book. (Questions 4–5)*
2. Students summarize their first 10 flips and their 100 flips on the *Coin Flipping Data Tables* Activity Page in the *Discovery Assignment Book. (Questions 6–7)*
3. Students pool their data to obtain results for 1000 flips and record their data on the *Coin Flipping Data Tables* Activity Page in the *Discovery Assignment Book. (Question 8)*

Part 2. Graphs

Students make and compare three graphs of their data. *(Questions 9–10)*

Part 3. Explore

Students list the possible outcomes when flipping two coins and list the ways 0, 1, and 2 heads can come up. They use the information to analyze their data. *(Questions 11–12)*

Part 4. Probability

1. Students record the probabilities of flipping 0, 1, and 2 heads on the *Comparing Probability with Results* Activity Page in the *Discovery Assignment Book. (Question 14)*
2. Students compare their experimental results with the probabilities using the Results of Coin Flipping table. *(Questions 15–17)*

Homework

1. *Questions 1–4* provide practice translating fractions, decimals, and percents. Assign these questions before students analyze their data.
2. Assign *Question 5* after students complete the lab. They play a game and use what they learn from the lab to decide if it is fair or unfair.
3. Assign Part 7 of the Home Practice.

Assessment

1. Assign points to one or more sections of the lab and grade them as an assessment.
2. As students analyze their group data, record their abilities to make and interpret bar graphs on the *Observational Assessment Record.*
3. Transfer appropriate documentation to students' *Individual Assessment Record Sheets.*

Answer Key is on pages 148–153.

Notes:

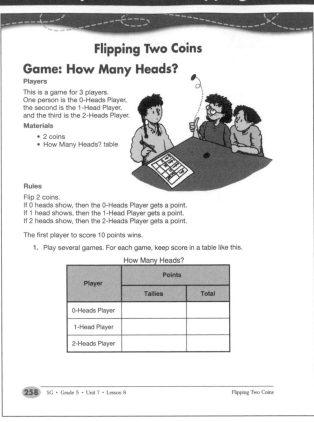

Student Guide - page 258

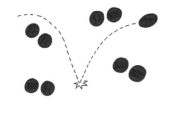

Student Guide - page 259

*Answers and/or discussion are included in the Lesson Guide.

Student Guide (pp. 258–259)

1.–2. Answers will vary.

3. This is not a mathematically fair game since the 1-Head player has a better chance of winning. There are two ways to get one head (first heads then tails or first tails then heads), but only one way to get no heads and only one way to get two heads.*

4. Answers will vary. See the Lesson Guide for sample data (Figures 28–31) and discussion of the questions.*

Student Guide (pp. 260–261)

5.–8. Answers will vary. See the Lesson Guide for sample data (Figures 28–31) and discussion of the questions.*

9. Bar graphs will make more sense. See Figures 32–34 for sample graphs.*

10. A. Answers will vary. Possible response based on sample data: The tallest bar is in the middle in all three graphs. The height of the bars is different in all three graphs.*

B. The middle bar—the bar for 1 head showing.

C. The tallest bar is twice as tall as the other two bars.

11. A. HH, HT, TH, TT*

B. One way: TT

C. Two ways: HT or TH

D. One way: HH

12. It explains that one head came up about twice as often as two heads or no heads.*

Data Tables

5. Now flip the penny and the nickel 100 times. Record your trials in the table on the *100 Two-Coin Flips* Activity Page in the *Discovery Assignment Book*. Write the outcome of the penny first and the nickel second. For example, if the penny shows heads and the nickel shows tails, then record HT in the outcome column.

100 Two-Coin Flips

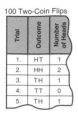

Trial	Outcome	Number of Heads
1.	HT	1
2.	HH	2
3.	TH	1
4.	TT	0
5.	TH	1

6. Look at the data for your first 10 trials only. Complete the 10-Trial Table on the *Coin Flipping Data Tables* Activity Page in the *Discovery Assignment Book* to show the number, fraction, and percent of the first 10 trials that have 0, 1, and 2 heads. The first row shows an example. Write your data in your table.

10-Trial Table

Number of Heads	N Number of Trials Out of 10	$\frac{N}{10}$ Fraction of Trials Out of 10	Equivalent Fraction with Denominator of 100	Percent of 10 Trials
0	3	$\frac{3}{10}$	$\frac{30}{100}$	30%
1				
2				

7. Look at the data from all 100 trials. Complete the 100-Trial Table on the *Coin Flipping Data Tables* Activity Page. Show the number, fraction, and percent of your 100 trials that have 0, 1, and 2 heads.

Student Guide - page 260

---

8. Now collect data from 10 groups to get a total of 1000 trials. Complete the 1000-Trial Table on the *Coin Flipping Data Tables* Activity Page. Show the number, fraction, and percent of 1000 trials that have 0, 1, and 2 heads.

9. Make 3 graphs—one for each of your data tables in Questions 6, 7, and 8.
- Plot the Number of Heads on the horizontal axis and the Percent of Trials on the vertical axis.
- Think about whether bar graphs or point graphs make more sense here.

10. Describe your graphs.
   A. How are they alike? How are they different?
   B. Which bar is the tallest?
   C. In the 1000-Trial Graph, how many times taller is the tallest bar than the other two bars?

11. A. What are the possible outcomes when you flip 2 coins? List them.
   B. How many ways can 0 heads come up? List the way(s).
   C. How many ways can 1 head come up? List the way(s).
   D. How many ways can 2 heads come up? List the way(s).

12. How does knowing the number of ways the coins can land help you to understand why the experiment (and your graphs) turned out the way they did?

Probability

The **probability** of 2 heads (HH) when two coins are flipped is the number of ways 2 heads can show, divided by the total number of ways the coins can land.

$$\text{Probability of 2 heads showing} = 1 \div 4 = \tfrac{1}{4}$$

The probability tells us about how often we can expect an event to occur when an experiment is repeated many times.

Student Guide - page 261

*Answers and/or discussion are included in the Lesson Guide.

13. Since the probability of 2 heads is one-fourth, we can expect 2 heads to show about one-fourth of the time, when we flip the coin many times. Did that happen in your experiment?

14. Use your answers to Question 11 to compute the probabilities of getting 0 heads and 1 head. Enter the probabilities in a probability table like the one below. Your copy is on the *Comparing Probability with Results* Activity Page in the *Discovery Assignment Book*.

Probabilities of Coin Flipping

Number of Heads	Ways Heads Can Come Up	Probability (as a fraction)	Probability (as a percent)
0			
1			
2	HH	$\frac{1}{4}$	25%

15. Use the Results of Coin Flipping table from the *Comparing Probability with Results* Activity Page. Enter the percents of the trials in your experiment that had 0, 1, and 2 heads. (Use the data from the last column of the tables in Questions 6, 7, and 8.)

Results of Coin Flipping

Number of Heads	Percent of 10 Trials	Percent of 100 Trials	Percent of 1000 Trials
0			
1			
2			

16. Compare your tables from Questions 14 and 15. What pattern do you see? Explain what is happening as more trials are made.

17. Do the results of your experiment match your predictions in Question 4? Why or why not?

Student Guide - page 262

Student Guide (p. 262)

13. Answers will vary.

14. See Figure 35 in Lesson Guide 8.*

15. Answers will vary. See Figure 36 in Lesson Guide 8 for sample data.*

16. Students will probably notice that as the number of trials increases, the results more closely approximate 25% chance of 0 heads, 50% chance of 1 head, and 25% chance of 2 heads.*

17. Answers will vary.

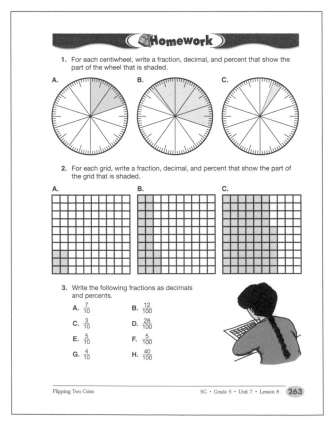

Student Guide - page 263

Student Guide (p. 263)

Homework

1. **A.** $\frac{20}{100}$ or $\frac{2}{10}$; 0.2 or 0.20; 20%

  B. $\frac{42}{100}$, 0.42, 42%

  C. $\frac{4}{100}$, 0.04, 4%

2. **A.** $\frac{6}{100}$, 0.06, 6%

  B. $\frac{23}{100}$, 0.23, 23%

  C. $\frac{66}{100}$, 0.66, 66%

3. **A.** 0.7, 70%

  B. 0.12, 12%

  C. 0.3, 30%

  D. 0.28, 28%

  E. 0.5, 50%

  F. 0.05, 5%

  G. 0.4, 40%

  H. 0.40, 40%

*Answers and/or discussion are included in the Lesson Guide.

Student Guide (p. 264)

4.

	Fraction	Decimal	Decimal to the Nearest Hundredth	Percent to the Nearest Percent
A.	$\frac{256}{1000}$	0.256	.26	26%
B.	$\frac{492}{1000}$	0.492	.49	49%
C.	$\frac{36}{1000}$	0.036	.04	4%
D.	$\frac{40}{1000}$	0.040	.04	4%
E.	$\frac{487}{1000}$	0.487	.49	49%

5. B. HH, HT, TH, TT*

C. Player 1 scores when the outcomes are HH or TT. Player 2 scores when the outcomes are HT or TH.

D. It is a fair game. Each player has an equal chance of winning. There are two ways of pennies matching (HH or TT) and two ways of pennies not matching (HT or TH).

Student Guide - page 264

Discovery Assignment Book (p. 99)

Home Practice†

Part 7. What's the Chance?

1. A. $\frac{5}{20}$ or $\frac{1}{4}$, 0.25, 25%

 B. $\frac{2}{20}$ or $\frac{1}{10}$, 0.1, or 0.10, 10%

 C. $\frac{3}{20}$, 0.15, 15%

 D. $\frac{7}{20}$, 0.35, 35%

 E. $\frac{3}{20}$, 0.15, 15%

2. Orange. The probability for picking the orange ball is the highest.

3. It is a good prediction because the probability of picking a red ball or an orange ball is $\frac{5}{20} + \frac{7}{20} = \frac{12}{20}$ or 60%.

Discovery Assignment Book - page 99

*Answers and/or discussion are included in the Lesson Guide.
†Answers for all the Home Practice in the *Discovery Assignment Book* are at the end of the unit.

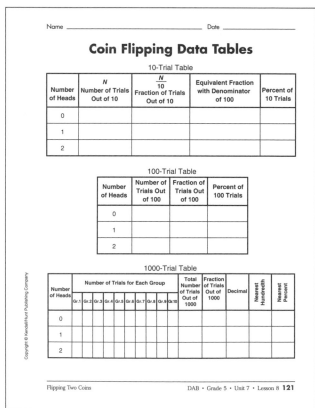

Discovery Assignment Book - page 119

Discovery Assignment Book (p. 119)

100 Two-Coin Flips*

See Figure 28 in Lesson Guide 8 for a sample data table.

Discovery Assignment Book - page 121

Discovery Assignment Book (p. 121)

Coin Flipping Data Tables*

See Figures 29–31 in Lesson Guide 8 for sample data tables.

---

*Answers and/or discussion are included in the Lesson Guide.

Discovery Assignment Book (p. 123)

Comparing Probability with Results*

See Figures 35–36 in Lesson Guide 8 for sample data tables.

Name _____ Date _____

Comparing Probability with Results

Probabilities of Coin Flipping

Number of Heads	Ways Heads Can Come Up	Probability (as a fraction)	Probability (as a percent)
0			
1			
2			

Results of Coin Flipping

Number of Heads	Percent of 10 Trials	Percent of 100 Trials	Percent of 1000 Trials
0			
1			
2			

Flipping Two Coins   DAB • Grade 5 • Unit 7 • Lesson 8 **123**

Discovery Assignment Book - page 123

---

*Answers and/or discussion are included in the Lesson Guide.

Families with Two Children

Estimated Class Sessions

1

Lesson Overview

This activity gives a real-world application of the coin-flipping model. Students investigate the various number of boys a family with two children might have and compute the probability of each number of boys. Then they make lists of families they know with 2 children, combine their lists to make a class list of 100 two-children families, and compare the number of families from this list that have 0, 1, and 2 boys with the numbers they predicted using probability.

Key Content

- Computing probabilities.
- Expressing probabilities as fractions and percents.
- Using probability to predict.
- Comparing probabilities with real-world data.

Homework

Students collect data at home on two-children families.

Materials List

Supplies and Copies

Student	Teacher
Supplies for Each Student	**Supplies**
Copies	**Copies/Transparencies**

All blackline masters including assessment, transparency, and DPP masters are also on the Teacher Resource CD.

Student Books

Families with Two Children (*Student Guide* Pages 265–267)

Teaching the Activity

Question 1 on the *Families with Two Children* Activity Pages in the *Student Guide* asks students to make a list of all the two-children families that are possible. They complete a data table as shown in Figure 37. They use the table to answer *Questions 2–3.* The table shows that 1 type of family has 0 boys (GG), 2 types of families have 1 boy (GB and BG), and 1 type of family has 2 boys (BB).

Types of Two-Children Families

First Child (Boy or Girl)	Second Child (Boy or Girl)
Boy	Boy
Girl	Boy
Boy	Girl
Girl	Girl

Figure 37: *Possible two-children families*

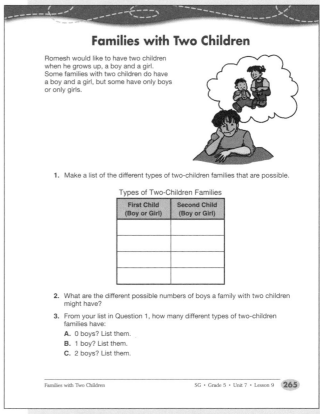

Families with Two Children

Romesh would like to have two children when he grows up, a boy and a girl. Some families with two children do have a boy and a girl, but some have only boys or only girls.

1. Make a list of the different types of two-children families that are possible.

Types of Two-Children Families

First Child (Boy or Girl)	Second Child (Boy or Girl)

2. What are the different possible numbers of boys a family with two children might have?

3. From your list in Question 1, how many different types of two-children families have:
   A. 0 boys? List them.
   B. 1 boy? List them.
   C. 2 boys? List them.

Families with Two Children   SG • Grade 5 • Unit 7 • Lesson 9   **265**

Student Guide - page 265 (*Answers on p. 158*)

Student Guide - page 266 (Answers on p. 158)

Student Guide - page 267 (Answers on p. 158)

Question 4 asks students to give the probability of having each type of family (if a family has two children). Since there are four possible ways to have a two-child family and one way to have no boys (GG), then the probability of having no boys is 1 out of 4 ($\frac{1}{4}$) or 25%. Using the same reasoning, there are 2 out of 4 ways to have 1 boy (GB and BG), so the probability of having one boy is $\frac{2}{4}$ or 50%. The probability of having 2 boys (BB) is $\frac{1}{4}$ or 25%.

Question 5 asks students to predict the number of families of each type they would expect in a sample of 100 families. Using the probabilities from *Question 4,* it is reasonable to predict that about $\frac{1}{4}$ or 25 of the families will have no boys, $\frac{1}{2}$ or 50 of the families will have 1 boy, and $\frac{1}{4}$ or 25 of the families will have 2 boys.

To complete *Questions 6–7,* the class compiles a list of families that have two children. Students can work in groups to list the families by name and record the number of boys in each family. Then the groups can pool the data for 100 families, tallying the number of families with 0, 1, and 2 boys.

To complete *Question 8,* students compare their data from *Question 7* to their predictions in *Question 5.* It is highly likely that the results will closely match the predictions in the discussion of *Question 4.* However, students should not expect *exactly* 25 two-boy families, 50 one-boy families, and 25 no-boy families. To conclude the discussion, ask students to compare the lab *Flipping Two Coins* in Lesson 8 to the Boys Per Family Survey in this lesson. How are they alike? How are they different?

Homework and Practice

For homework, students can ask their family members or neighbors to list two-children families they know. Then they can add the information for these families to their data table for *Question 6.*

Teaching the Activity

1. Students answer *Questions 1–5* on the *Families with Two Children* Activity Pages in the *Student Guide* to make predictions about the number of families, out of 100 two-children families, that have 0, 1, and 2 boys.

2. In *Questions 6–8* students generate a class list of 100 two-children families they know. They compare this data with their predictions.

Homework

Students collect data at home on two-children families.

Answer Key is on page 158.

Notes:

Families with Two Children

Romesh would like to have two children when he grows up, a boy and a girl. Some families with two children do have a boy and a girl, but some have only boys or only girls.

1. Make a list of the different types of two-children families that are possible.

Types of Two-Children Families

First Child (Boy or Girl)	Second Child (Boy or Girl)

2. What are the different possible numbers of boys a family with two children might have?

3. From your list in Question 1, how many different types of two-children families have:
   A. 0 boys? List them.
   B. 1 boy? List them.
   C. 2 boys? List them.

Families with Two Children   SG • Grade 5 • Unit 7 • Lesson 9   **265**

Student Guide - page 265

Student Guide (pp. 265–267)

1. Types of Two-Children Families *

First Child (Boy or Girl)	Second Child (Boy or Girl)
Boy	Boy
Girl	Boy
Boy	Girl
Girl	Girl

2. 0 boys, 1 boy, 2 boys*

3. A. One type: GG*
   B. Two types: BG, GB
   C. One type: BB

4.* A. $\frac{1}{4}$, 25%   B. $\frac{2}{4}$ or $\frac{1}{2}$, 50%
   C. $\frac{1}{4}$, 25%

5.* A. 25   B. 50
   C. 25

6.–8. Answers will vary.*

---

4. If a family has two children:
   A. What is the probability of having 0 boys? Express as a fraction and as a percent. *Hint:* The probability of 0 boys is
   $$\frac{\text{the number of types of families with 0 boys}}{\text{the number of types of families with 2 children}}$$
   B. What is the probability of having 1 boy? Express as a fraction and as a percent.
   C. What is the probability of having 2 boys? Express as a fraction and as a percent.

5. If you sampled 100 families that have two children, about how many of them would you expect to have:
   A. 0 boys?
   B. 1 boy?
   C. 2 boys?

Testing Your Predictions
Compare the two-children families that you and your classmates know with the predictions you made in Question 5.

6. Think of some families you know that have two children—perhaps your family or the families of your neighbors or relatives. Don't include families of other students in the class. List them in a table like the table below.

Boys Per Family

Family Name	Children	Number of Boys
Jones	BB	2
Young	BG	1
Jackson	GG	0
Clinton	BB	2
Martinez	GB	1

266 SG • Grade 5 • Unit 7 • Lesson 9   Families with Two Children

Student Guide - page 266

7. Combine your list of families with your classmates' lists until you have a list of 100 families that have two children. (Be sure not to list the same families more than once.) Make a table like the one below.

Two-Children Families We Know

Number of Boys	Number of Families (out of 100)	Percent of Families
0		
1		
2		

8. How do your results compare with your predictions from Question 5?

Families with Two Children   SG • Grade 5 • Unit 7 • Lesson 9   **267**

Student Guide - page 267

*Answers and/or discussion are included in the Lesson Guide.

Unlikely Heroes

Estimated Class Sessions

Lesson Overview

I

Unlikely Heroes is a story about John Kerrich and Eric Christensen and the probability experiments they carried out while in prison during World War II. Kerrich and Christensen explored what happens when a coin is flipped many times. They recorded their explorations in data tables and graphed their results. After the war, Kerrich published the results of the experiments in a book.

Note: This book is historical fiction. While elements of this story are factual, the actual unfolding of the story is fiction.

Key Content

- Exploring the probabilities involved in flipping a coin.
- Discussing fair and unfair coin tosses.
- Connecting mathematics to real-world events.
- Interpreting graphs.

Key Vocabulary

- fair
- unfair

Materials List

Supplies and Copies

Student	Teacher
Supplies for Each Student • pennies, optional	**Supplies**
Copies	**Copies/Transparencies**

All blackline masters including assessment, transparency, and DPP masters are also on the Teacher Resource CD.

Student Books
Unlikely Heroes (*Adventure Book* Pages 35–46)

Daily Practice and Problems and Home Practice
DPP items Y–Z (*Unit Resource Guide* Page 28)

Note: Classrooms whose pacing differs significantly from the suggested pacing of the units should use the Math Facts Calendar in Section 4 of the *Facts Resource Guide* to ensure students receive the complete math facts program.

Daily Practice and Problems

Suggestions for using the DPPs are on page 165.

Y. Bit: Adding and Subtracting Fractions (URG p. 28)

A. $\frac{3}{5} + \frac{3}{10} =$ B. $\frac{7}{8} - \frac{1}{2} =$

C. $\frac{1}{6} + \frac{1}{3} =$ D. $\frac{1}{2} - \frac{1}{3} =$

Z. Task: Practice (URG p. 28)

Solve the following using paper and pencil.
Estimate to be sure your answers are reasonable.

A. $836 + 47 =$ B. $2058 - 1467 =$

C. $66 \times 33 =$ D. $7399 \div 8 =$

E. $4702 \div 7 =$ F. $3967 - 1098 =$

Pages 36–37

Encourage students to find a book of world records.

Adventure Book - page 36

Adventure Book - page 37

Adventure Book - page 38

Adventure Book - page 39

Historical Note

John Kerrich, a South African mathematician and an English citizen, was living in Copenhagen, Denmark, when World War II broke out. He and his friend, Eric Christensen, were imprisoned when the Germans invaded Denmark just two days before John Kerrich was scheduled to fly to England. Kerrich spent the remainder of the war as a political prisoner in a Danish prison. It was at this prison that Kerrich and Christensen carried out probability experiments.

Page 40

- *What do you think happens when a coin is flipped many times?*

- *What happened when you flipped a coin in Lesson 7 Flipping One Coin?*

If the coin is a **fair** coin, the distribution of heads and tails will get closer to 50% heads/50% tails when flipped many times. If the coin is an **unfair** coin, it will land more often on heads or tails when flipped many times.

- *Why might Christensen have said that the coin-flipping experiment sounds boring?*

Christensen probably said the experiment sounded boring since he already knew the outcome. The coin would land on heads half the time and tails the other half.

Adventure Book - page 40

Page 41

- *Why might Kerrich have gotten 4 heads and 6 tails when flipping the coin ten times? How do their results compare with your results from Flipping One Coin (Lesson 7)?*

Students should recall that when flipping a fair coin ten times, they could get 4 heads and 6 tails. But, if the coin is fair, 5 heads and 5 tails is a little more likely. The Law of Large Numbers says that if we flip the coin many times, heads will show half the time and tails will show half the time. Ten flips is not a large number of flips.

- *Do you think that Kerrich is flipping a fair coin?*

You can't tell yet. You have to keep flipping.

Adventure Book - page 41

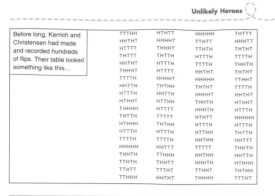

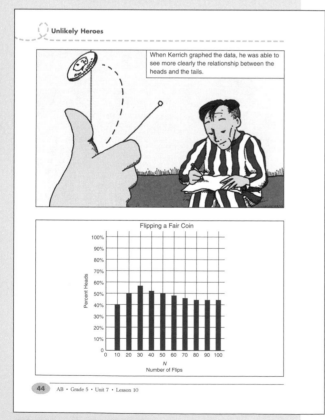

Adventure Book - page 43

Adventure Book - page 44

Page 43

- *Look at the data table. What do you notice about the percents of heads and tails flipped as the number of flips gets larger?*

- *Look at the data table. What is the percent of heads for N = 10 flips? N = 20 flips? N = 100 flips? N = 1000 flips? N = 10,000 flips?*

For $N = 100$ flips, the percent of heads equals 44%, for $N = 1000$ flips the percent of heads equals 50%, and for $N = 10,000$ flips, the percent of heads equals 49%.

As the number of flips increases, the percents of heads and tails flipped approach 50% each.

Page 44

- *Tell a story for the graph. What would the graph look like if you graphed the data for all 10,000 flips?*

The graph shows the percent of heads for the first 100 flips. It starts with 40% heads when $N = 10$, increases to about 55% when $N = 30$, then decreases to about 45% when $N = 80$ to $N = 100$. If the horizontal axis extended to 10,000 flips, the bars would level off and stay very near the 50% level. You may want to sketch this on the board for students.

Page 45

- *Predict what might happen when Kerrich flips the lead-weighted coin 10,000 times.*

Predictions will vary. One possible prediction is that the lead side will land down most of the time.

- *Tell a story for the graph of the lead-weighted coin.*

Stories will vary. However, students should see by the graph that the lead side will probably land down between 70%–80% of the time. After 30 flips the lead side was down between 70%–80% of the time. After 80 flips, the percent of "lead side down" was getting close to 72% or 73%.

- *Is the coin with lead attached a fair coin? Explain.*

It is an unfair coin because the lead side has a higher probability of landing down, so heads and tails are not equally likely events.

Homework and Practice

DPP items Y and Z provide computation practice with fractions and whole numbers.

Literature Connections

Students may be interested in reading about children's experiences during World War II. Louis Lowry's *Number the Stars* is a story about a Jewish girl's experiences while hiding in Denmark during World War II.

- Lowry, Louis. *Number the Stars.* Houghton Mifflin Co., Boston, MA, 1989.

Resource

Kerrich, J.E. *An Experimental Introduction to the Theory of Probability.* Einar Munksgaard, Copenhagen, Denmark, 1946.

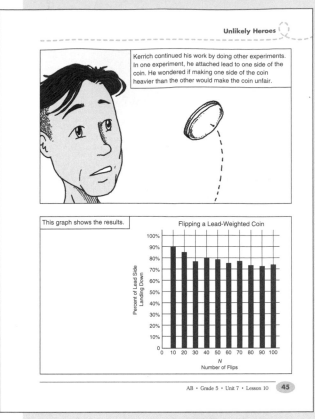

Adventure Book - page 45

Name _____ Date _____

Unit 7 Home Practice

PART 1 *Triangle Flash Cards: All the Facts*
Look at your *Multiplication* and *Division Facts I Know* charts. Take home your *Triangle Flash Cards* for all the facts you have not circled. With the help of a family member, use the cards to study a small group of facts (8 to 10 facts) each night.

Ask a family member to choose one flash card at a time. To quiz you on a multiplication fact, he or she should cover the corner containing the highest number. Multiply the two uncovered numbers.

To quiz you on a division fact, your family member can cover one of the smaller numbers. (One of the smaller numbers is circled. The other has a square around it.) Use the two uncovered numbers to solve a division fact.

Ask your family member to mix up the multiplication and division facts. He or she should sometimes cover the highest number, sometimes cover the circled number, and sometimes cover the number in the square.

PART 2 Practicing the Operations
Solve the following problems using paper and pencil. Estimate to be sure your answers are reasonable.

A. $248 + 275 =$ B. $8208 - 775 =$ C. $26 \times 54 =$

D. $893 \times 5 =$ E. $9 \overline{\smash{)}11{,}346}$ F. $3 \overline{\smash{)}1748}$

DECIMALS AND PROBABILITY   DAB • Grade 5 • Unit 7   **97**

Discovery Assignment Book - page 97

Name _____ Date _____

PART 3 Fractions, Decimals, and Percents
Fill in the chart, writing each number as a fraction, a decimal, and a percent. The first one is done for you. Use your centiwheel if you need to.

	Fraction	Decimal	Percent			Fraction	Decimal	Percent
A.	$\frac{1}{4}$	.25	25%	F.		$\frac{20}{100}$		
B.		.98		G.			1.00	
C.	$\frac{5}{100}$			H.		$\frac{1}{100}$		
D.			16%	I.				75%
E.		.50		J.				7%

PART 4 Adding Fractions
Solve the following problems.

A. $\frac{1}{2} + \frac{1}{4} =$ B. $\frac{1}{2} + \frac{3}{4} =$

C. $\frac{1}{2} + \frac{1}{3} =$ D. $\frac{1}{2} + \frac{2}{3} =$

E. $\frac{1}{3} + \frac{1}{4} =$ F. $\frac{2}{3} + \frac{3}{4} =$

PART 5 Reading, Writing, and Ordering Decimals
Write the following numbers as decimals and then put them in order from smallest to largest.

A. thirty-seven thousandths _____

B. two hundred forty-two and four-hundredths _____

C. one hundred nine and fourteen-thousandths _____

D. six hundred sixteen-thousandths _____

98   DAB • Grade 5 • Unit 7   DECIMALS AND PROBABILITY

Discovery Assignment Book - page 98

Discovery Assignment Book (pp. 97–98)

Part 2. Practicing the Operations

A. 523   B. 7433
C. 1404   D. 4465
E. 1260 R6   F. 582 R2

Part 3. Fractions, Decimals, and Percents

	Fraction	Decimal	Percent
A.	$\frac{1}{4}$	.25	25%
B.	$\frac{98}{100}$	.98	98%
C.	$\frac{5}{100}$	.05	5%
D.	$\frac{16}{100}$	.16	16%
E.	$\frac{1}{2}, \frac{5}{10},$ or $\frac{50}{100}$	.50	50%

	Fraction	Decimal	Percent
F.	$\frac{20}{100}$	.20	20%
G.	$\frac{100}{100} = 1$	1.00	100%
H.	$\frac{1}{100}$	.01	1%
I.	$\frac{3}{4}$ or $\frac{75}{100}$	.75	75%
J.	$\frac{7}{100}$	.07	7%

Part 4. Adding Fractions

A. $\frac{3}{4}$

B. $\frac{5}{4}$ or $1\frac{1}{4}$

C. $\frac{5}{6}$

D. $\frac{7}{6}$ or $1\frac{1}{6}$

E. $\frac{7}{12}$

F. $\frac{17}{12}$ or $1\frac{5}{12}$

Part 5. Reading, Writing, and Ordering Decimals

A. .037

B. 242.04

C. 109.014

D. 0.616

.037, 0.616, 109.014, 242.04

Discovery Assignment Book (pp. 99–100)

Part 6. Working with Decimals

A. 57.95

B. 0.803

C. 3.56

D. 6.77

E. 39.84

F. 0.134

G. 176.785

H. 327.64

I. 0.22885

Part 7. What's the Chance?

I. **A.** $\frac{5}{20}$ or $\frac{1}{4}$, 0.25, 25%

    B. $\frac{2}{20}$ or $\frac{1}{10}$, 0.1, or 0.10, 10%

    C. $\frac{3}{20}$, 0.15, 15%

    D. $\frac{7}{20}$, 0.35, 35%

    E. $\frac{3}{20}$, 0.15, 15%

2. Orange. The probability for picking the orange ball is the highest.

3. It is a good prediction because the probability of picking a red ball or an orange ball is $\frac{5}{20} + \frac{7}{20} = \frac{12}{20}$ or 60%.

Part 8. The Swim Meet

I. 47.41 seconds

2. **A.** 3 minutes and 15.33 seconds

    B. 200 meters

3. 13.11 seconds

4. **A.** 300 meters

    B. Answers will vary. One possible estimate is $1\frac{1}{2}$ min + $\frac{1}{2}$ min + $\frac{1}{2}$ min + $\frac{1}{2}$ min + 1 min or about 4 min.

5. 8 hours and 15 minutes

6. $10.50

7. Estimates will vary. One possible estimate is: $600 \times 10¢ = 6000¢$ or $60.00.

Name _____ Date _____

PART 6 **Working with Decimals**
Solve the following problems using paper and pencil. Estimate to be sure your answers are reasonable.

  A. 45.6 + 12.35 =   **B.** 0.76 + 0.043 =   **C.** 0.89 × 4 =

  D. 7.3 − 0.53 =   **E.** 4.8 × 8.3 =   **F.** 0.67 × 2 =

  G. 176.4 + 0.385 =   **H.** 456.07 − 128.43 =   **I.** 4.577 × 0.5 =

PART 7 **What's the Chance?**
Manny works at the miniature golf range. The owner bought 20 new balls. He bought 5 red balls, 2 white balls, 3 green balls, 7 orange balls, and 3 yellow balls. Manny put all the new balls in a bucket. In between customers, he tries a probability experiment. If Manny picks one ball, the probability that he will pick a yellow ball is $\frac{3}{20}$.

  1. Without looking, he picks one ball from the bucket. Write each of the following probabilities as a fraction, decimal, and percent:
    A. The probability that he will pick a red ball.
    B. The probability that he will pick a white ball.
    C. The probability that he will pick a green ball.
    D. The probability that he will pick an orange ball.

  2. What color ball will Manny most likely pick? Justify your answer.

  3. Manny predicts that he will choose a red ball or an orange ball. Is this a good prediction? Why or why not?

DECIMALS AND PROBABILITY   DAB • Grade 5 • Unit 7 **99**

Discovery Assignment Book - page 99

Name _____ Date _____

PART 8 **The Swim Meet**
Choose an appropriate method to solve each of the following problems. For some questions you may need to find an exact answer, while for others you may only need an estimate. For each question, you may choose to use paper and pencil, mental math, or a calculator. Use a separate sheet of paper to explain how you solved each problem.

  1. Shannon is on the swim team. She swam the backstroke in 7 meets. Her times for each race were 53.19 seconds, 49.67 seconds, 47.30 seconds, 43.86 seconds, 46.07 seconds, 45.87 seconds, and 45.91 seconds. What was Shannon's average speed for the backstroke during these meets? (Use the mean.)

  2. A four-person team is needed to swim the medley relay. Each team member swims 50 meters using a different stroke. During one relay, Lin swam 50 meters using the butterfly stroke in 59.53 seconds, Shannon swam the backstroke in 46.12 seconds, Blanca swam the breaststroke in 53.27 seconds, and Grace finished with the freestyle stroke in 36.41 seconds.
    A. How many minutes and seconds did it take the team to complete the entire relay?
    B. What is the total distance that the relay team swam?

  3. During the first swim meet of the season, Frank swam the 50-meter breaststroke event in 57.62 seconds. During the final meet of the season, he swam the 50-meter breaststroke in 44.51 seconds. How many seconds faster did Frank swim the 50-meter breaststroke at the end of the season than at the beginning?

  4. During one swim meet Edward swam in 5 different events. He swam the 100-meter individual medley in 1 minute 38.30 seconds, the 50-meter butterfly in 42.48 seconds, the 50-meter breaststroke in 44.80 seconds, the 50-meter freestyle in 32.83 seconds, and the 50-meter backstroke in 45.87 seconds.
    A. How many meters did he swim during this meet?
    B. About how many minutes did Edward spend swimming during this meet?

  5. The final swim meet of the season began at 8:30 A.M. It ended at 4:45 P.M. How long was the swim meet?

  6. Parents held a bake sale during each meet to raise money for the team. During one meet, the parents sold cupcakes for $.25 each. They sold 42 cupcakes. How much money did they get for the cupcakes?

  7. The ribbons for the winners cost $.08 each. During the swim season the team used 648 ribbons. About how much did the team spend on the ribbons for this season?

100 DAB • Grade 5 • Unit 7   DECIMALS AND PROBABILITY

Discovery Assignment Book - page 100

Glossary

This glossary provides definitions of key vocabulary terms in the Grade 5 lessons. Locations of key vocabulary terms in the curriculum are included with each definition. Components Key: URG = *Unit Resource Guide* and SG = *Student Guide.*

A

Acute Angle (URG Unit 6; SG Unit 6)
An angle that measures less than 90°.

Acute Triangle (URG Unit 6 & Unit 15; SG Unit 6 & Unit 15)
A triangle that has only acute angles.

All-Partials Multiplication Method (URG Unit 2)
A paper-and-pencil method for solving multiplication problems. Each partial product is recorded on a separate line. (*See also* partial product.)

$$\begin{array}{r} 186 \\ \times\ 3 \\ \hline 18 \\ 240 \\ 300 \\ \hline 558 \end{array}$$

Altitude of a Triangle (URG Unit 15; SG Unit 15)
A line segment from a vertex of a triangle perpendicular to the opposite side or to the line extending the opposite side; also, the length of this line. The altitude is also called the height of the triangle.

Angle (URG Unit 6; SG Unit 6)
The amount of turning or the amount of opening between two rays that have the same endpoint.

Arc (URG Unit 14; SG Unit 14)
Part of a circle between two points. (*See also* circle.)

Area (URG Unit 4 & Unit 15; SG Unit 4 & Unit 15)
A measurement of size. The area of a shape is the amount of space it covers, measured in square units.

Average (URG Unit 1 & Unit 4; SG Unit 1 & Unit 4)
A number that can be used to represent a typical value in a set of data. (*See also* mean, median, and mode.)

Axes (URG Unit 10; SG Unit 10)
Reference lines on a graph. In the Cartesian coordinate system, the axes are two perpendicular lines that meet at the origin. The singular of axes is axis.

B

Base of a Triangle (URG Unit 15; SG Unit 15)
One of the sides of a triangle; also, the length of the side. A perpendicular line drawn from the vertex opposite the base is called the height or altitude of the triangle.

Base of an Exponent (URG Unit 2; SG Unit 2)
When exponents are used, the number being multiplied. In $3^4 = 3 \times 3 \times 3 \times 3 = 81$, the 3 is the base and the 4 is the exponent. The 3 is multiplied by itself 4 times.

Base-Ten Pieces (URG Unit 2; SG Unit 2)
A set of manipulatives used to model our number system as shown in the figure below. Note that a skinny is made of 10 bits, a flat is made of 100 bits, and a pack is made of 1000 bits.

Base-Ten Shorthand (URG Unit 2)
A graphical representation of the base-ten pieces as shown below.

Nickname	Picture	Shorthand
bit	▫	·
skinny	▭	/
flat		
pack		

Benchmarks (SG Unit 7)
Numbers convenient for comparing and ordering numbers, e.g., $0, \frac{1}{2}, 1$ are convenient benchmarks for comparing and ordering fractions.

Best-Fit Line (URG Unit 3; SG Unit 3)
The line that comes closest to the points on a point graph.

Binning Data (URG Unit 8; SG Unit 8)
Placing data from a data set with a large number of values or large range into intervals in order to more easily see patterns in the data.

Bit (URG Unit 2; SG Unit 2)
A cube that measures 1 cm on each edge.
It is the smallest of the base-ten pieces and
is often used to represent 1. (*See also* base-ten pieces.)

C

Cartesian Coordinate System (URG Unit 10;
SG Unit 10)
A method of locating points on a flat surface by means of an ordered pair of numbers. This method is named after its originator, René Descartes. (*See also* coordinates.)

Categorical Variable (URG Unit 1; SG Unit 1)
Variables with values that are not numbers. (*See also* variable and value.)

Center of a Circle (URG Unit 14; SG Unit 14)
The point such that every point on a circle is the same distance from it. (*See also* circle.)

Centiwheel (URG Unit 7; SG Unit 7)
A circle divided into 100 equal sections used in exploring fractions, decimals, and percents.

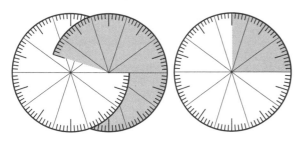

Central Angle (URG Unit 14; SG Unit 14)
An angle whose vertex is at the center of a circle.

Certain Event (URG Unit 7; SG Unit 7)
An event that has a probability of 1 (100%).

Chord (URG Unit 14; SG Unit 14)
A line segment that connects two points on a circle.
(*See also* circle.)

Circle (URG Unit 14; SG Unit 14)
A curve that is made up of all the points that are the same distance from one point, the center.

Circumference (URG Unit 14; SG Unit 14)
The distance around a circle.

Common Denominator (URG Unit 5 & Unit 11;
SG Unit 5 & Unit 11)
A denominator that is shared by two or more fractions.
A common denominator is a common multiple of the denominators of the fractions. 15 is a common denominator of $\frac{2}{3} (= \frac{10}{15})$ and $\frac{4}{5} (= \frac{12}{15})$ since 15 is divisible by both 3 and 5.

Common Fraction (URG Unit 7; SG Unit 7)
Any fraction that is written with a numerator and denominator that are whole numbers. For example, $\frac{3}{4}$ and $\frac{9}{4}$ are both common fractions. (*See also* decimal fraction.)

Commutative Property of Addition (URG Unit 2)
The order of the addends in an addition problem does not matter, e.g., $7 + 3 = 3 + 7$.

Commutative Property of Multiplication (URG Unit 2)
The order of the factors in a multiplication problem does not matter, e.g., $7 \times 3 = 3 \times 7$. (*See also* turn-around facts.)

Compact Method (URG Unit 2)
Another name for what is considered the traditional multiplication algorithm.

$$\begin{array}{r} {}^{2}{}^{1}186 \\ \times\ 3 \\ \hline 558 \end{array}$$

Composite Number (URG Unit 11; SG Unit 11)
A number that has more than two distinct factors. For example, 9 has three factors (1, 3, 9) so it is a composite number.

Concentric Circles (URG Unit 14; SG Unit 14)
Circles that have the same center.

Congruent (URG Unit 6 & Unit 10; SG Unit 6)
Figures that are the same shape and size. Polygons are congruent when corresponding sides have the same length and corresponding angles have the same measure.

Conjecture (URG Unit 11; SG Unit 11)
A statement that has not been proved to be true, nor shown to be false.

Convenient Number (URG Unit 2; SG Unit 2)
A number used in computation that is close enough to give a good estimate, but is also easy to compute with mentally, e.g., 25 and 30 are convenient numbers for 27.

Convex (URG Unit 6)
A shape is convex if for any two points in the shape, the line segment between the points is also inside the shape.

Coordinates (URG Unit 10; SG Unit 10)
An ordered pair of numbers that locates points on a flat surface relative to a pair of coordinate axes. For example, in the ordered pair (4, 5), the first number (coordinate) is the distance from the point to the vertical axis and the second coordinate is the distance from the point to the horizontal axis. (*See also* axes.)

Corresponding Parts (URG Unit 10; SG Unit 10)
Matching parts in two or more figures. In the figure below, Sides AB and A′B′ are corresponding parts.

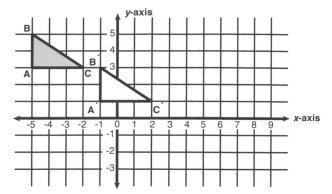

Cryptography (SG Unit 11) The study of secret codes.

Cubic Centimeter (URG Unit 13)
The volume of a cube that is one centimeter long on each edge.

D

Data (SG Unit 1)
Information collected in an experiment or survey.

Decagon (URG Unit 6; SG Unit 6)
A ten-sided, ten-angled polygon.

Decimal (URG Unit 7; SG Unit 7)
1. A number written using the base ten place value system.
2. A number containing a decimal point.

Decimal Fraction (URG Unit 7; SG Unit 7)
A fraction written as a decimal. For example, 0.75 and 0.4 are decimal fractions and $\frac{75}{100}$ and $\frac{4}{10}$ are the equivalent common fractions.

Degree (URG Unit 6; SG Unit 6)
A degree (°) is a unit of measure for angles. There are 360 degrees in a circle.

Denominator (URG Unit 3; SG Unit 3)
The number below the line in a fraction. The denominator indicates the number of equal parts in which the unit whole is divided. For example, the 5 is the denominator in the fraction $\frac{2}{5}$. In this case the unit whole is divided into five equal parts. (*See also* numerator.)

Density (URG Unit 13; SG Unit 13)
The ratio of an object's mass to its volume.

Diagonal (URG Unit 6)
A line segment that connects nonadjacent corners of a polygon.

Diameter (URG Unit 14; SG Unit 14)
1. A line segment that connects two points on a circle and passes through the center.
2. The length of this line segment.

Digit (SG Unit 2)
Any one of the ten symbols 0, 1, 2, 3, 4, 5, 6, 7, 8, 9. The number 37 is made up of the digits 3 and 7.

Dividend (URG Unit 4 & Unit 9; SG Unit 4 & Unit 9)
The number that is divided in a division problem, e.g., 12 is the dividend in 12 ÷ 3 = 4.

Divisor (URG Unit 2, Unit 4, & Unit 9; SG Unit 2, Unit 4, & Unit 9)
In a division problem, the number by which another number is divided. In the problem 12 ÷ 4 = 3, the 4 is the divisor, the 12 is the dividend, and the 3 is the quotient.

Dodecagon (URG Unit 6; SG Unit 6)
A twelve-sided, twelve-angled polygon.

E

Endpoint (URG Unit 6; SG Unit 6)
The point at either end of a line segment or the point at the end of a ray.

Equally Likely (URG Unit 7; SG Unit 7)
When events have the same probability, they are called equally likely.

Equidistant (URG Unit 14)
At the same distance.

Equilateral Triangle (URG Unit 6, Unit 14, & Unit 15)
A triangle that has all three sides equal in length. An equilateral triangle also has three equal angles.

Equivalent Fractions (URG Unit 3; SG Unit 3)
Fractions that have the same value, e.g., $\frac{2}{4} = \frac{1}{2}$.

Estimate (URG Unit 2; SG Unit 2)
1. To find *about* how many (as a verb).
2. A number that is *close to* the desired number (as a noun).

Expanded Form (SG Unit 2)
A way to write numbers that shows the place value of each digit, e.g., 4357 = 4000 + 300 + 50 + 7.

Exponent (URG Unit 2 & Unit 11; SG Unit 2 & Unit 11)
The number of times the base is multiplied by itself. In $3^4 = 3 \times 3 \times 3 \times 3 = 81$, the 3 is the base and the 4 is the exponent. The 3 is multiplied by itself 4 times.

Extrapolation (URG Unit 13; SG Unit 13)
Using patterns in data to make predictions or to estimate values that lie beyond the range of values in the set of data.

F

Fact Families (URG Unit 2; SG Unit 2)
Related math facts, e.g., 3 × 4 = 12, 4 × 3 = 12, 12 ÷ 3 = 4, 12 ÷ 4 = 3.

Factor Tree (URG Unit 11; SG Unit 11)
A diagram that shows the prime factorization of a number.

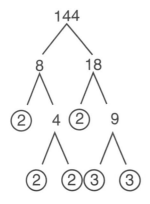

Factors (URG Unit 2 & Unit 11; SG Unit 2 & Unit 11)
1. In a multiplication problem, the numbers that are multiplied together. In the problem $3 \times 4 = 12$, 3 and 4 are the factors.
2. Numbers that divide a number evenly, e.g., 1, 2, 3, 4, 6, and 12 are all the factors of 12.

Fair Game (URG Unit 7; SG Unit 7)
A game in which it is equally likely that any player will win.

Fewest Pieces Rule (URG Unit 2)
Using the least number of base-ten pieces to represent a number. (*See also* base-ten pieces.)

Fixed Variables (URG Unit 4; SG Unit 3 & Unit 4)
Variables in an experiment that are held constant or not changed, in order to find the relationship between the manipulated and responding variables. These variables are often called controlled variables. (*See also* manipulated variable and responding variable.)

Flat (URG Unit 2; SG Unit 2)
A block that measures 1 cm $\times$ 10 cm $\times$ 10 cm. It is one of the base-ten pieces and is often used to represent 100. (*See also* base-ten pieces.)

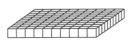

Flip (URG Unit 10; SG Unit 10)
A motion of the plane in which the plane is reflected over a line so that any point and its image are the same distance from the line.

Forgiving Division Method
(URG Unit 4; SG Unit 4)
A paper-and-pencil method for division in which successive partial quotients are chosen and subtracted from the dividend, until the remainder is less than the divisor. The sum of the partial quotients is the quotient. For example, $644 \div 7$ can be solved as shown at the right.

```
          92
      7 ) 644
          140  | 20
          ----
          504
          350  | 50
          ----
          154
          140  | 20
          ----
           14
           14  |  2
          ----
            0  | 92
```

Formula (SG Unit 11 & Unit 14)
A number sentence that gives a general rule. A formula for finding the area of a rectangle is Area = length $\times$ width, or $A = l \times w$.

Fraction (URG Unit 7; SG Unit 7)
A number that can be written as a/b where a and b are whole numbers and b is not zero.

G

Googol (URG Unit 2)
A number that is written as a 1 with 100 zeroes after it (10^{100}).

Googolplex (URG Unit 2)
A number that is written as a 1 with a googol of zeroes after it.

H

Height of a Triangle (URG Unit 15; SG Unit 15)
A line segment from a vertex of a triangle perpendicular to the opposite side or to the line extending the opposite side; also, the length of this line. The height is also called the altitude.

Hexagon (URG Unit 6; SG Unit 6)
A six-sided polygon.

Hypotenuse (URG Unit 15; SG Unit 15)
The longest side of a right triangle.

I

Image (URG Unit 10; SG Unit 10)
The result of a transformation, in particular a slide (translation) or a flip (reflection), in a coordinate plane. The new figure after the slide or flip is the image of the old figure.

Impossible Event (URG Unit 7; SG Unit 7)
An event that has a probability of 0 or 0%.

Improper Fraction (URG Unit 3; SG Unit 3)
A fraction in which the numerator is greater than or equal to the denominator. An improper fraction is greater than or equal to one.

Infinite (URG Unit 2)
Never ending, immeasurably great, unlimited.

Interpolation (URG Unit 13; SG Unit 13)
Making predictions or estimating values that lie between data points in a set of data.

Intersect (URG Unit 14)
To meet or cross.

Isosceles Triangle (URG Unit 6 & Unit 15)
A triangle that has at least two sides of equal length.

J

K

L

Lattice Multiplication
(URG Unit 9; SG Unit 9)
A method for multiplying that
uses a lattice to arrange the
partial products so the digits are
correctly placed in the correct
place value columns. A lattice
for 43 × 96 = 4128 is shown at
the right.

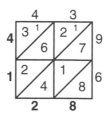

Legs of a Right Triangle (URG Unit 15; SG Unit 15)
The two sides of a right triangle that form the right angle.

Length of a Rectangle (URG Unit 4 & Unit 15; SG Unit 4 & Unit 15)
The distance along one side of a rectangle.

Line
A set of points that form a straight path extending infinitely in two directions.

Line of Reflection (URG Unit 10)
A line that acts as a mirror so that after a shape is flipped over the line, corresponding points are at the same distance (equidistant) from the line.

Line Segment (URG Unit 14)
A part of a line between and including two points, called the endpoints.

Liter (URG Unit 13)
Metric unit used to measure volume. A liter is a little more than a quart.

Lowest Terms (SG Unit 11)
A fraction is in lowest terms if the numerator and denominator have no common factor greater than 1.

M

Manipulated Variable (URG Unit 4; SG Unit 4)
In an experiment, the variable with values known at the beginning of the experiment. The experimenter often chooses these values before data is collected. The manipulated variable is often called the independent variable.

Mass (URG Unit 13)
The amount of matter in an object.

Mean (URG Unit 1 & Unit 4; SG Unit 1 & Unit 4)
An average of a set of numbers that is found by adding the values of the data and dividing by the number of values.

Measurement Division (URG Unit 4)
Division as equal grouping. The total number of objects and the number of objects in each group are known. The number of groups is the unknown. For example, tulip bulbs come in packages of 8. If 216 bulbs are sold, how many packages are sold?

Median (URG Unit 1; SG Unit 1)
For a set with an odd number of data arranged in order, it is the middle number. For an even number of data arranged in order, it is the mean of the two middle numbers.

Meniscus (URG Unit 13)
The curved surface formed when a liquid creeps up the side of a container (for example, a graduated cylinder).

Milliliter (ml) (URG Unit 13)
A measure of capacity in the metric system that is the volume of a cube that is one centimeter long on each side.

Mixed Number (URG Unit 3; SG Unit 3)
A number that is written as a whole number followed by a fraction. It is equal to the sum of the whole number and the fraction.

Mode (URG Unit 1; SG Unit 1)
The most common value in a data set.

Mr. Origin (URG Unit 10; SG Unit 10)
A plastic figure used to represent the origin of a coordinate system and to indicate the directions of the x- and y- axes. (and possibly the z-axis).

N

N-gon (URG Unit 6; SG Unit 6)
A polygon with N sides.

Negative Number (URG Unit 10; SG Unit 10)
A number less than zero; a number to the left of zero on a horizontal number line.

Nonagon (URG Unit 6; SG Unit 6)
A nine-sided polygon.

Numerator (URG Unit 3; SG Unit 3)
The number written above the line in a fraction. For example, the 2 is the numerator in the fraction $\frac{2}{5}$. In this case, we are interested in two of the five parts. (*See also* denominator.)

Numerical Expression (URG Unit 4; SG Unit 4)
A combination of numbers and operations, e.g., $5 + 8 \div 4$.

Numerical Variable (URG Unit 1; SG Unit 1)
Variables with values that are numbers. (*See also* variable and value.)

O

Obtuse Angle (URG Unit 6; SG Unit 6)
An angle that measures more than 90°.

Obtuse Triangle (URG Unit 6 & Unit 15; SG Unit 6 & Unit 15)
A triangle that has an obtuse angle.

Octagon (URG Unit 6; SG Unit 6)
An eight-sided polygon.

Ordered Pair (URG Unit 10; SG Unit 10)
A pair of numbers that gives the coordinates of a point on a grid in relation to the origin. The horizontal coordinate is given first; the vertical coordinate is given second. For example, the ordered pair (5, 3) gives the coordinates of the point that is 5 units to the right of the origin and 3 units up.

Origin (URG Unit 10; SG Unit 10)
The point at which the *x*- and *y*-axes intersect on a coordinate plane. The origin is described by the ordered pair (0, 0) and serves as a reference point so that all the points on the plane can be located by ordered pairs.

P

Pack (URG Unit 2; SG Unit 2)
A cube that measures 10 cm on each edge. It is one of the base-ten pieces and is often used to represent 1000. (*See also* base-ten pieces.)

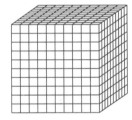

Parallel Lines (URG Unit 6 & Unit 10)
Lines that are in the same direction. In the plane, parallel lines are lines that do not intersect.

Parallelogram (URG Unit 6)
A quadrilateral with two pairs of parallel sides.

Partial Product (URG Unit 2)
One portion of the multiplication process in the all-partials multiplication method, e.g., in the problem 3 × 186 there are three partial products: 3 × 6 = 18, 3 × 80 = 240, and 3 × 100 = 300. (*See also* all-partials multiplication method.)

Partitive Division (URG Unit 4)
Division as equal sharing. The total number of objects and the number of groups are known. The number of objects in each group is the unknown. For example, Frank has 144 marbles that he divides equally into 6 groups. How many marbles are in each group?

Pentagon (URG Unit 6; SG Unit 6)
A five-sided polygon.

Percent (URG Unit 7; SG Unit 7)
Per hundred or out of 100. A special ratio that compares a number to 100. For example, 20% (twenty percent) of the jelly beans are yellow means that out of every 100 jelly beans, 20 are yellow.

Perimeter (URG Unit 15; SG Unit 15)
The distance around a two-dimensional shape.

Period (SG Unit 2)
A group of three places in a large number, starting on the right, often separated by commas as shown at the right.

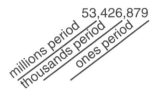

Perpendicular Lines (URG Unit 14 & Unit 15; SG Unit 14)
Lines that meet at right angles.

Pi (π) (URG Unit 14; SG Unit 14)
The ratio of the circumference to diameter of a circle. π = 3.14159265358979. . . . It is a nonterminating, nonrepeating decimal.

Place (SG Unit 2)
The position of a digit in a number.

Place Value (URG Unit 2; SG Unit 2)
The value of a digit in a number. For example, the 5 is in the hundreds place in 4573, so it stands for 500.

Polygon (URG Unit 6; SG Unit 6)
A two-dimensional connected figure made of line segments in which each endpoint of every side meets with an endpoint of exactly one other side.

Population (URG Unit 1 Unit 1)
A collection of persons or things whose properties will be analyzed in a survey or experiment.

Portfolio (URG Unit 2; SG Unit 2)
A collection of student work that show how a student's skills, attitudes, and knowledge change over time.

Positive Number (URG Unit 10; SG Unit 10)
A number greater than zero; a number to the right of zero on a horizontal number line.

Power (URG Unit 2; SG Unit 2)
An exponent. Read 10^4 as, "ten to the fourth power" or "ten to the fourth." We say 10,000 or 10^4 is the fourth power of ten.

Prime Factorization (URG Unit 11; SG Unit 11)
Writing a number as a product of primes. The prime factorization of 100 is 2 × 2 × 5 × 5.

Prime Number (URG Unit 11; SG Unit 11)
A number that has exactly two factors: itself and 1. For example, 7 has exactly two distinct factors, 1 and 7.

Probability (URG Unit 7; SG Unit 1 & Unit 7)
A number from 0 to 1 (0% to 100%) that describes how likely an event is to happen. The closer that the probability of an event is to one, the more likely the event will happen.

Product (URG Unit 2; SG Unit 2)
The answer to a multiplication problem. In the problem $3 \times 4 = 12$, 12 is the product.

Proper Fraction (URG Unit 3; SG Unit 3)
A fraction in which the numerator is less than the denominator. Proper fractions are less than one.

Proportion (URG Unit 3 & Unit 13; SG Unit 13)
A statement that two ratios are equal.

Protractor (URG Unit 6; SG Unit 6)
A tool for measuring angles.

Q

Quadrants (URG Unit 10; SG Unit 10)
The four sections of a coordinate grid that are separated by the axes.

Quadrilateral (URG Unit 6; SG Unit 6)
A polygon with four sides. (*See also* polygon.)

Quotient (URG Unit 4 & Unit 9; SG Unit 2, Unit 4, & Unit 9)
The answer to a division problem. In the problem $12 \div 3 = 4$, the 4 is the quotient.

R

Radius (URG Unit 14; SG Unit 14)
1. A line segment connecting the center of a circle to any point on the circle.
2. The length of this line segment.

Ratio (URG Unit 3 & Unit 12; SG Unit 3 & Unit 13)
A way to compare two numbers or quantities using division. It is often written as a fraction.

Ray (URG Unit 6; SG Unit 6)
A part of a line with one endpoint that extends indefinitely in one direction.

Rectangle (URG Unit 6; SG Unit 6)
A quadrilateral with four right angles.

Reflection (URG Unit 10)
(*See* flip.)

Regular Polygon (URG Unit 6; SG Unit 6; DAB Unit 6)
A polygon with all sides of equal length and all angles equal.

Remainder (URG Unit 4 & Unit 9; SG Unit 4 & Unit 9)
Something that remains or is left after a division problem. The portion of the dividend that is not evenly divisible by the divisor, e.g., $16 \div 5 = 3$ with 1 as a remainder.

Repeating Decimals (SG Unit 9)
A decimal fraction with one or more digits repeating without end.

Responding Variable (URG Unit 4; SG Unit 4)
The variable whose values result from the experiment. Experimenters find the values of the responding variable by doing the experiment. The responding variable is often called the dependent variable.

Rhombus (URG Unit 6; SG Unit 6)
A quadrilateral with four equal sides.

Right Angle (URG Unit 6; SG Unit 6)
An angle that measures 90°.

Right Triangle (URG Unit 6 & Unit 15; SG Unit 6 & Unit 15)
A triangle that contains a right angle.

Rubric (URG Unit 1)
A scoring guide that can be used to guide or assess student work.

S

Sample (URG Unit 1)
A part or subset of a population.

Scalene Triangle (URG Unit 15)
A triangle that has no sides that are equal in length.

Scientific Notation (URG Unit 2; SG Unit 2)
A way of writing numbers, particularly very large or very small numbers. A number in scientific notation has two factors. The first factor is a number greater than or equal to one and less than ten. The second factor is a power of 10 written with an exponent. For example, 93,000,000 written in scientific notation is 9.3×10^7.

Septagon (URG Unit 6; SG Unit 6)
A seven-sided polygon.

Side-Angle-Side (URG Unit 6 & Unit 14)
A geometric property stating that two triangles having two corresponding sides with the included angle equal are congruent.

Side-Side-Side (URG Unit 6)
A geometric property stating that two triangles having corresponding sides equal are congruent.

Sides of an Angle (URG Unit 6; SG Unit 6)
The sides of an angle are two rays with the same endpoint. (*See also* endpoint and ray.)

Sieve of Eratosthenes (SG Unit 11)
A method for separating prime numbers from nonprime numbers developed by Eratosthenes, an Egyptian librarian, in about 240 BCE.

Similar (URG Unit 6; SG Unit 6)
Similar shapes have the same shape but not necessarily the same size.

Skinny (URG Unit 2; SG Unit 2)
A block that measures 1 cm × 1 cm × 10 cm.
It is one of the base-ten pieces
and is often used to represent 10.
(*See also* base-ten pieces.)

Slide (URG Unit 10; SG Unit 10)
Moving a geometric figure in the plane by moving every point of the figure the same distance in the same direction. Also called translation.

Speed (URG Unit 3 & Unit 5; SG Unit 3 & Unit 5)
The ratio of distance moved to time taken, e.g., 3 miles/1 hour or 3 mph is a speed.

Square (URG Unit 6 & Unit 14; SG Unit 6)
A quadrilateral with four equal sides and four right angles.

Square Centimeter (URG Unit 4; SG Unit 4)
The area of a square that is 1 cm long on each side.

Square Number (URG Unit 11)
A number that is the product of a whole number multiplied by itself. For example, 25 is a square number since 5 × 5 = 25. A square number can be represented by a square array with the same number of rows as columns. A square array for 25 has 5 rows of 5 objects in each row or 25 total objects.

Standard Form (SG Unit 2)
The traditional way to write a number, e.g., standard form for three hundred fifty-seven is 357. (*See also* expanded form and word form.)

Standard Units (URG Unit 4)
Internationally or nationally agreed-upon units used in measuring variables, e.g., centimeters and inches are standard units used to measure length and square centimeters and square inches are used to measure area.

Straight Angle (URG Unit 6; SG Unit 6)
An angle that measures 180°.

T

Ten Percent (URG Unit 4; SG Unit 4)
10 out of every hundred or $\frac{1}{10}$.

Tessellation (URG Unit 6 & Unit 10; SG Unit 6)
A pattern made up of one or more repeated shapes that completely covers a surface without any gaps or overlaps.

Translation
(*See* slide.)

Trapezoid (URG Unit 6)
A quadrilateral with exactly one pair of parallel sides.

Triangle (URG Unit 6; SG Unit 6)
A polygon with three sides.

Triangulating (URG Unit 6; SG Unit 6)
Partitioning a polygon into two or more nonoverlapping triangles by drawing diagonals that do not intersect.

Turn-Around Facts (URG Unit 2)
Multiplication facts that have the same factors but in a different order, e.g., 3 × 4 = 12 and 4 × 3 = 12. (*See also* commutative property of multiplication.)

Twin Primes (URG Unit 11; SG Unit 11)
A pair of prime numbers whose difference is 2. For example, 3 and 5 are twin primes.

U

Unit Ratio (URG Unit 13; SG Unit 13)
A ratio with a denominator of one.

V

Value (URG Unit 1; SG Unit 1)
The possible outcomes of a variable. For example, red, green, and blue are possible values for the variable *color*. Two meters and 1.65 meters are possible values for the variable *length*.

Variable (URG Unit 1; SG Unit 1)
1. An attribute or quantity that changes or varies. (*See also* categorical variable and numerical variable.)
2. A symbol that can stand for a variable.

Variables in Proportion (URG Unit 13; SG Unit 13)
When the ratio of two variables in an experiment is always the same, the variables are in proportion.

Velocity (URG Unit 5; SG Unit 5)
Speed in a given direction. Speed is the ratio of the distance traveled to time taken.

Vertex (URG Unit 6; SG Unit 6)
A common point of two rays or line segments that form an angle.

Volume (URG Unit 13)
The measure of the amount of space occupied by an object.

W

Whole Number
Any of the numbers 0, 1, 2, 3, 4, 5, 6 and so on.

Width of a Rectangle (URG Unit 4 & Unit 15; SG Unit 4 & Unit 15)
The distance along one side of a rectangle is the length and the distance along an adjacent side is the width.

Word Form (SG Unit 2)
A number expressed in words, e.g., the word form for 123 is "one hundred twenty-three." (*See also* expanded form and standard form.)

X

Y

Z